Wha .... ~~,~~.ɩɡ aɒout

Christianity Expanding Into Universal Spirituality

All religions evolve, and Christianity is evolving rapidly today. Don MacGregor's book is a lucid and thoughtful guide to this process, and shows how the essential core teachings of Christianity can be disentangled from unhelpful interpretations that stand in the way of a living Christian faith in the twenty-first century. I found this book stimulating and inspiring. It is also admirably brief and clear.

Dr Rupert Sheldrake, biologist and author of *The Science Delusion* and other titles

With his deep and extensive understanding of Christianity and Perennial Wisdom teachings, Don MacGregor shares in this lucid, profound and wonderfully compassionate book that they, and indeed all major spiritual traditions, are; 'the path of the evolution of human consciousness'. Fluent in both science and spirituality, he shows how their emerging convergence is revealing universal consciousness as the fundamental nature of reality. Vitally, *Expanding Christianity* gifts its readers with a revitalisation of Jesus' call to love one another and affirms that we have now reached the stage in our collective evolution when we can begin to do so on a global level.

Dr Jude Currivan, cosmologist, author of *The Cosmic Hologram* and co-founder of *WholeWorld-View*

This is a really helpful and stimulating book for anyone interested in the future of the Church and Christianity. Concise, easy to read and full of helpful insights it combines a classical understanding of theology with all the new awarenesses of a contemporary holistic approach. If I had a magic wand, every clergyperson would read it, as well as every pagan and witch with space in their heart for the Christian message.

William Bloom, educator and author of *The Power of Modern Spirituality* and Director of the Spiritual Companions Trust

Don MacGregor's vision of an expanded framework of wisdom Christianity consonant with modern scientific insights is a fitting articulation for our times with its emphasis on inner transformation rather than sacrificial belief. It encourages us to live life in its fullness of love and compassion and provides a blueprint for an engaged and ecological spirituality in our journey towards wholeness and integration.

David Lorimer, Programme Director, Scientific and Medical Network

It seems that humanity is currently undergoing a significant evolutionary shift which will involve all institutions in significant change. Revd Don MacGregor was ahead of the curve with his publication of *Blue Sky God* and now this small book provides us with a more detailed understanding of the steps that Christianity can take towards embracing more recent knowledge and understanding without any loss of the original teachings. This contribution towards a more universal spiritualty will help fulfil the wish of Jesus the Christ that 'you will be One'.

Janice Dolley, co-author *Christian Evolution : Moving towards a Global Spirituality* and *Awakening to a New Reality; Conscious Conversations across the Horizon of Death*

This book offers the reader a window into the perennial principles that are foundational to the Christian faith. With remarkable clarity, the author provides an insightful view of the Christian perspective, and how it must evolve to meet the spiritual needs of modern-day humanity. It is a must-read for anyone who believes that Christianity has to expand its framework to include the new discoveries arising within science, cosmology and the study of human consciousness.

William Meader, International Speaker and author of *Shine Forth: The Soul's Magical Destiny* Portland, Oregon, USA

While media often focus on the decline of religion or the excessive fervour of fundamentalism, Don MacGregor addresses the shifting Christian consciousness of our time, inviting us to outgrow former beliefs in favour of newly expanding horizons that are both inspiring and promising. This book provides a timely reassurance for those troubled or confused by such massive and rapid change.

Fr Diarmuid O'Murchu, R.C.Priest, social psychologist and author of *Quantum Theology* and many other titles

Christianity Expanding Into Universal Spirituality

THE WISDOM SERIES BOOK 1

Christianity Expanding Into Universal Spirituality

THE WISDOM SERIES BOOK 1

Don MacGregor

CHRISTIAN ALTERNATIVE
BOOKS

Winchester, UK
Washington, USA

JOHN HUNT PUBLISHING

First published by Christian Alternative Books, 2020
Christian Alternative Books is an imprint of John Hunt Publishing Ltd.,
No. 3 East St., Alresford, Hampshire SO24 9EE, UK
office@jhpbooks.com
www.johnhuntpublishing.com
www.christian-alternative.com

For distributor details and how to order please visit the 'Ordering' section on our website.

Text copyright: Don MacGregor 2019

ISBN: 978 1 78904 422 5
978 1 78904 423 2 (ebook)
Library of Congress Control Number: 2019952949

A CIP catalogue record for this book is available from the British Library.

Design: Stuart Davies

UK: Printed and bound by CPI Group (UK) Ltd, Croydon, CR0 4YY
US: Printed and bound by Thomson-Shore, 7300 West Joy Road, Dexter, MI 48130

We operate a distinctive and ethical publishing philosophy in
all areas of our business, from our global network of authors to
production and worldwide distribution.

Contents

Previous Titles by the author

Blue Sky God: The Evolution of Science and Christianity. Circle
Books, 2012
ISBN 978-1-84694-937-1

Introduction

Big pictures need a framework to hold them. The framework that held Christianity for 1500 years was the medieval worldview of God as a supreme being who was in charge of our fate and the occurrences that happened in our daily life. If the crops were good, God was pleased with us. If we won a war, God was on our side. If there was a flood, God was punishing us. It was a simple, graspable, understandable concept for times when the vast majority of humanity had no education and were illiterate. This framework retained power in the hands of the few: the leaders, the priests, the religious hierarchy. But, in the West, along came the Reformation in the sixteenth century and then the Enlightenment in the seventeenth. This influx of creative energy brought the printing press, new scientific understanding, education and a huge challenge to the medieval viewpoint. For the last 500 years, this has been working out in society, with huge upheavals, revolutions and developments. Science has taken over from religious dogma, and has developed its own dogma of scientific materialism. Technology has advanced by leaps and bounds to the stage of world domination. Astronomy has emerged from and eclipsed astrology. Christianity has stuck, largely, to its medieval framework. This still works for some, who remain in the churches, defending the sandcastle on the beach against the incoming tide. And there are many parts of the world where the medieval worldview still exists, along with the feudal system, and Christianity flourishes there in that mindset.

But for those of us who have woken up to the pulsating energetic universe, with all its size and utter complexity, we need a bigger framework. Christian theology has to have a larger cosmology in which it can begin to explore new meanings and paths in order to make sense of the present and future of humanity. Science is now telling us that everything is energetically interconnected in one interpenetrating whole and holographic universe. We are One with a Whole that is so vast, so complex, so far beyond our understanding that we find it difficult to believe that this One Life, this One Consciousness could concern itself with us. But we are part of that One Consciousness. Our minds are part of the Great Mind. Our very form, our bodies, our emotions, our thoughts are part of that Whole. We are individually held in being as drops within the ocean of God.

That is the bigger framework that I believe Christianity, and all other religious beliefs and spiritualities, are moving into, slowly and haltingly. The framework has been held down through the centuries by a tradition that goes by a number of names – the Perennial Philosophy, the Ageless Wisdom, Esoteric Philosophy. Strands of it can be traced back to the Greek philosophers, to the early Hindu texts, to the Egyptian mystery religions. It is there in the Jewish Kabbalah and the writings of the Christian mystics. It is esoteric in that it has been veiled, hidden within the traditions, like an underground stream of living water flowing until it emerges from the rock. Revd Dr. Cynthia Bourgeault describes it nicely in the introduction to her book *The Wisdom Way of Knowing.*

When I use the term Wisdom, I am designating a precise and comprehensive science of spiritual transformation that has existed since the headwaters of the great world religions and is in fact their common ground... The Wisdom cosmology is bold, spacious and remarkably contemporary... It's remarkable how, no matter what spiritual path you pursue, the nuts and bolts of transformation end up looking pretty much the same; surrender, detachment, compassion, forgiveness. Whether you are a Christian, a Buddhist, a Jew, a Sufi, or a sannyasin, you will still go through the same eye of the needle to get where your true heart lies...

Through a series of books, I plan to explore the application of this larger cosmology to Christianity. In this first book, I am setting the scene for further writing to enlarge the exploration. It is set out in six short chapters, each one setting out something of the challenge to traditional Christian doctrine and theology that developed in the first thousand years after Jesus the Christ walked the land. At the end of each chapter are questions for reflection, a practice to try out, and recommended books and websites for further study.

Chapter 1

Why Should Christianity Change?

I started on a Christian path in 1983, in what I then thought of as a conversion experience, but now would call an awakening to love. I was involved with a large charismatic evangelical church in Leicester, with some lovely people, and I remember the first service I went to there, on Easter Sunday 1983. There was a lot of standing up and sitting down, reciting strange words and singing hymns, and it all struck me as rather weird. I hadn't been to church since I was nine, and then it was a dour, Presbyterian place that seemed very joyless. But it wasn't all the strange liturgy and singing that struck me, it was the conversations after and the love shown to us by the people. I suppose this cynical world these days would call it being 'love-bombed' but for me it was a real heart-warming experience and made me return there week in week out. Later that year came the real outpouring of love upon me that I call my true awakening.

I have worshipped in huge evangelical churches with 500 on a Sunday morning, sung and played in worship bands, led crazy youth services, been in charge of small inner city churches with an oppressed congregation, and looked after several rural churches in what I would call terminal decline. But throughout my Christian journey, I have struggled with the church teaching. Part of the reason why is that for a few years prior to this I had studied various teachings of what is variously called the 'Ageless Wisdom' or 'Perennial Wisdom' or 'Esoteric Philosophy'. This body of teaching gives an undergirding to all religious traditions, to the human psycho-spiritual makeup and to the whole metaphysical understanding of the universe and its working. No small claim then, but that teaching has undergirded my understanding of Christianity and helped to expand it into something for this twenty-first century. So this little book is the first of a series in which I hope to chart a path towards a more universal understanding of Christianity.

Consequently, this book is *not* for those who are entirely satisfied with their faith as expressed in the doctrines and liturgy of the Church. It *is* for the many millions in the Western world who have found it all too difficult to accept and are rejecting the institution and its patterns. That is a great sadness because I believe that, hiding in the depths of Christianity, there is still a very relevant and challenging spiritual path – but it means seeing and understanding things in a different way.

When I was a curate in a large evangelical church, I remember the vicar saying to me, 'I'd like to hear you preaching a sermon on the wrath of God.' My response was, 'You'll never hear that from me, because I don't believe in the wrath of God!' I openly admit I've struggled as a priest within the Anglican Church, both in England and in Wales. Its liturgy and doctrine stem from outmoded ways of thinking. There are aspects I value and enjoy – the singing, the quiet, the symbology, the prayers. But equally there are parts of even these that I struggle with – the wording of some hymns, the use of outmoded forms of address, the acceptance without any challenge of statements of belief like the Nicene Creed, which was formulated in 325CE. At one stage in my life as a vicar, I was called in by the Bishop to be asked if I could still say the Nicene Creed and mean it. To which my reply was yes, providing I could interpret it in my own way. Take this section, for example:

I believe in one Lord, Jesus Christ,
the only Son of God,
eternally begotten of the Father,
God from God, Light from Light,
true God from true God,
begotten, not made,

of one Being with the Father.
Through him all things were made.

Who are we talking about here? Not the human body of Jesus of Nazareth. No human body is eternal. So is it something like an eternal divine creative energy? What do we mean by 'eternal Son'? And 'begotten, not made'? How can everything be made through this 'being'? Are Jesus and the Christ exactly the same? The density of this creed needs a huge amount of unpacking, interpretation and theological understanding. Simply reciting it on a Sunday does nothing to help us understand what we are saying. Plus the creed says nothing about how we should live our lives, absolutely nothing, yet that surely is the most important thing, to be changed by the path we follow, so that the world becomes a better place. On reflection, maybe I should have asked the bishop to explain it all!

Back in 2005, I wrote what I thought should be recited in Church instead of the creed:

The Christian Way

Christians are called, in God's strength and love and following the example of Christ Jesus, to walk in the light, which means:

- To love and care for one another, not to ignore or be indifferent or to hate.
- To be generous with each other, to look after those in need, not to be selfish, uncaring, or hard of heart.
- To forgive each other, not to harbour grudges, bitterness or resentment.
- To live in peace and harmony, not to look for conflict, or to seek violence, revenge and retribution.
- To live honest, truthful lives, having integrity in our daily living, not to cheat, not to tread on others, not to stab in the back.

6

- To seek justice for others, to speak out, to challenge unfair systems, not to hide our heads in the sand.
- To be stewards of God's creation, caring for the biosphere in which we exist.
- To heal and make whole, to work for a better world in which to live.
- To be joyful, to rejoice in life and in God.

This is the Way of Christ, the way of the kingdom of God, of which Jesus spoke so often.

But, of course, it is not permissible for a member of the clergy to use anything like that in place of the creed in the Church of England or in Wales. So I've struggled with the traditions. These are some of the issues I have wrestled with. Maybe you have too.

- The concept of an almighty, all-powerful, distant and remote God.
- The doctrine of Jesus the man as the *only-begotten* Son, hardly human at all.
- The idea that the death of Jesus appeases the wrath of an angry God.
- The emphasis that God is 'up there' and not 'in here'.
- Suffering and an all-powerful God who 'allows' it to happen.
- The idea of heaven as an eternal reward and hell as an eternal punishment.
- The confusing joining of Jesus and the Christ to make Jesus Christ.

I think most of these issues stem from one-sided distortions of teachings that originated in the first millennium and that need much more depth and understanding. They come from earlier ways of looking at the world, from a different paradigm or worldview. So why should Christianity change? The simple answer is that the Christian faith as presented in most churches today does not fit with today's world. It's not kept up with our understanding of life and the universe. It's not about punishment and sin. It's not about going to hell or heaven. It's about awakening and transformation. That was the essential message of Jesus. 'Repent!' meaning 'Change the way you think!' The form of Christianity created by the church has distracted us from his message, and the essence of that message is that we are to be transformed into the sort of person that Jesus of Nazareth had become.

I've called this book *Christianity Expanding* because I believe that is what the Christian faith has to do – to expand and transcend some of its traditional church teaching towards a more progressive and twenty-first-century understanding, a continuation of the initial inspired teaching of Jesus. It must move away from the concept that we are being saved from the wrathful punishment of a just but punitive God by the death of one man, to the idea that one man has blazed a transformational path for us all to follow, a path of self-emptying and surrender of the lower human nature. In the series of short books of which this is the first, I hope to set out something of that path, which is the path of the evolution of human consciousness.

I intend to chart a path from traditional Christianity to a more universal way of viewing it, more in line with the Perennial Philosophy teachings. I would like to emphasise that this is not a denial but rather a re-statement of the original teachings of Jesus. I believe many church doctrines have become stale and crystallised in form and need reinvigorating with an understanding of the world of today. Those doctrines have been valuable in the past, they have been the scaffolding that has held truths and a structure through some very difficult periods in human history, and so they are to be respected as part of the tradition. But the simple truth is that every other area of human thinking has moved on in the last five hundred years, and many new areas of thought have emerged. Why should that not apply to religious teachings as well? Is our God only a God of the medieval mentality, or is the divine agenda much, much bigger than that?

Chrysalis Christianity

One way of looking at what is happening to Christianity is to use an analogy of how the caterpillar changes into a butterfly. We have had recent experience of this, camping in France during a caterpillar infestation. The little blighters were up in the oak tree canopy, munching merrily on oak leaves. As they munched, they excreted little pellets like peppercorns which rained down on our tent. They also chomped their way through the leaf stalks and fell down with the leaves, so every night when they were most active, there was a constant patter of oak leaves, caterpillars and their poo on our tent! Needless to say, we moved the tent out from under the canopy of oaks. While we were there, it was obvious that the caterpillars were getting bigger and fatter, and as we left, they were beginning to pupate – but we don't know what they would have hatched out as. This infestation was over many miles of oak forest, so it would have been quite a sight when they all hatched out!

Reflecting on our experience, caterpillars feed and grow, feed more and grow more, and can shed their skin numerous times as they do so. They are constantly redefining their boundaries. But then comes a stage when a major transformation has to happen. This is an inevitable process and the caterpillar has no more control over it than we have of hair growing in various places on our bodies during our teens! The caterpillar stops moving, stops growing and develops a hard outer shell, a *chrysalis*. Everything inside the outer layer turns to goo! Well, actually, not quite everything. The essential mechanism for breathing, for life, stays in the same place and gets bigger – because in order to fly, a butterfly needs more oxygen than a caterpillar. The amazing

9

thing is that inside the caterpillar are structures called imaginal discs that do nothing at all for a caterpillar. But during the metamorphosis of the goo inside the chrysalis, these imaginal discs grow and develop into all the structures which the adult butterfly needs. A total transformation happens in order for the next stage to take off, literally. It's all there in potential in the caterpillar. There's the old joke about the two caterpillars talking to each other, when one looks up and sees a butterfly flying overhead. 'You wouldn't get me up in one of those,' he says! The point of the joke being that the change is inevitable, unstoppable. It will happen.

So let's think about 'Chrysalis Christianity'! It has grown and shed its skin numerous times. Theological trends and differences in practice have come and gone. It's grown bigger and bigger. But in the Western world, that growth has stopped. It's become crystallised, no longer able to keep up with the contemporary world. Its theological structures make it irrelevant for many, the doctrines and dogmas that have sustained it for two thousand years are not holding it any longer. The container has hardened. But inside the crystallised form, a new creature is beginning to take shape. Its imaginal discs are developing. Patches of future potential have been held within the faith until the time is right for them to develop – and they are now waking up. Like the caterpillar, it's reforming so that it can eventually take flight. Its basis is the caterpillar of tradition, but it looks and behaves very differently. It flies! It expands into another realm of understanding and being. The butterfly has a totally different view of the world, from an entirely different perspective. Its total transformation is based on its earlier life yet looks and feels completely different.

What is the new perspective for Christianity? Something is emerging. The teachings of Jesus were essentially about spiritual transformation and this vital message seems to have been submerged over the years of traditional Church teaching.

It became like an imaginal disc within the caterpillar of church teaching. It is part of the perennial wisdom tradition which can be traced back through the ages to pre-Christian times. My aim is to show that there is a wider, more spacious wisdom path within the body of Christian teaching that is about the transformation of the human being to be 'filled with all the fullness of God' (Ephesians 3:19). The Apostle Peter says it as well, that we are '...to become participants in the divine nature' (2 Peter 1:4). The teachings of Jesus were essentially about this path of transformation, not a transaction between God and humanity. It is about growing into the reality of Fullness and Oneness of the Divine – we are all One in the Divine Being that holds everything, sustains everything – and is everything.

Change Is Inevitable

There have been enormous changes in society over the last five hundred years and Christianity hasn't kept up with those changes in its theology and doctrine. Despite many progressive and reforming theologians hoping to move it on, the Church and its liturgy and practice appear to be stuck in a medieval time warp of first millennium thinking. The Christianity that is laid out before us in the Church has become a struggle for many to accept, whichever denomination we belong or used to belong to.

I am not wanting to change the essential essence of Christian teaching. Much of the teaching is still of great value and guides people along right pathways. But many of the concepts and doctrines come from a worldview which is far from our own, and that has misdirected the Church. For example, we no longer think of God as the kindly old bearded gent or autocratic dictator up in the clouds, yet it is the image that is still there in much of the liturgy, hymns and prayers that we use. For example, take this hymn:

Praise to the Lord, who doth prosper thy work and defend

11

thee;
Surely His goodness and mercy here daily attend thee:
Ponder anew, what the Almighty can do,
Who with His love doth befriend thee.

This lovely hymn tune reinforces the idea that God is entirely separate from us, caring for us and befriending us, but not within us, not infusing and transforming us. It contradicts the prayer of Jesus in John chapter 17 that we are all to be one and also the words attributed to St Paul in Ephesians 3:19 that we are all to be filled to the fullness of God.

Or there is the image of a vengeful, wrathful God who will punish us for stepping out of line. Some of the hymns and modern songs are beautiful and uplifting, but some contain wording which totally jars with our modern senses. For example, in the well-known hymn 'O worship the King, all glorious above' we read in verse two 'His chariots of wrath the deep thunder-clouds form, and dark is His path on the wings of the storm.' It's a great tune, but this is primitive religion, thinking that natural events are caused by God and then attributing the human emotion of wrath and anger to God. The sad truth is that many people take it literally. In many modern evangelical songs we often sing that God's wrath is in some way appeased by Jesus' death. The idea, called penal substitution, is that a sinless Saviour has to die to satisfy the righteous wrath of a totally just but ruthless God. It is a neat formula, but I think bears little resemblance to reality. It is also a barbaric notion, killing for forgiveness.

Another example of misdirection is the famous Bible verse that says 'For God so loved the world that he gave his only Son, so that everyone who believes in him may not perish but may have eternal life.' (John 3:16). 'Gave' is usually taken to mean 'sacrificed', but a brief look at the Greek wording shows that it could justifiably be translated as 'he brought forth his only Son.' God *brought forth* Jesus in order to show us how human beings can truly be. He was a forerunner, a trailblazer for a fuller humanity. On top of that, we can add in that the 'only Son' has a deeper hidden meaning. At Jesus' baptism, the wisdom teaching tells us that the Cosmic Christ became one with Jesus the man to enable him in his years of ministry. He became empowered by the third aspect of God, the love-wisdom of God. The early Church, steeped as it was in the Jewish sacrificial worship culture, soon interpreted Jesus' death purely as a sacrifice and sidelined the understanding of his life as the forerunner for us all, demonstrating the path we are all called to.

One of the problems is that we have so absorbed the idea that 'God is above, in the heavenly realms' that we see no room for the divine in our own realm, in our own being. The first line of the Lord's Prayer emphasises that viewpoint, 'Our Father, who art in heaven.' Immediately, we may get images of God up there in his home called heaven, separate from us. There are other expressions of this prayer that draw on the imagery in the original language of Aramaic that Jesus spoke. Aramaic is a much more poetic language with fewer words than Greek or English, so each word contains more nuances of meaning. Translating Aramaic into Greek or English means we have to choose just one word out of several that express something of the meaning in Aramaic, but in choosing just one word, much of the broader meaning is lost. The first line of the Lord's Prayer could become 'O Breath of Life, present in all dimensions of being.' Quite a difference in terminology, but the same concept behind it, that there is a Divine Being who is present with us. (To see a contemporary expression of the prayer, drawing on the Aramaic, see the end of the chapter.)

The teaching of the Church is that God is both transcendent and immanent, is both above and within creation. But the 'above and separate' notion is emphasised to the detriment of the inner divinity. Yet there are numerous Bible verses attributed to St Paul which speak of the immanent God.

Do you not know that you are God's temple and that God's Spirit dwells in you? (1 Corinthians 3:16)

I pray that you may have the power to comprehend, with all the saints, what is the breadth and length and height and depth, and to know the love of Christ that surpasses knowledge, so that you may be filled with all the fullness of God. (Ephesians 3:18–19)

To them God chose to make known how great among the Gentiles are the riches of the glory of this mystery, which is Christ in you, the hope of glory. (Colossians 1:27)

Guard the good treasure entrusted to you, with the help of the Holy Spirit living in us. (2 Timothy 1:14)

The Wisdom teaching (about which much more will be said in later books in this series) takes this a step further, that we are all *in* God, *in* Christ, and as such are all an aspect of the Divine. *En Christos* is a favourite expression of St Paul in his letters. This teaching has been retained within the Eastern Orthodox Church in the doctrine of Theosis or Divinisation of the human being. We find it stated boldly, in the terms of the time, in many of the writings of the early Church Fathers:

St Irenaeus of Lyons stated that God 'became what we are in order to make us what he is himself.'
St Clement of Alexandria says that 'he who obeys the Lord and follows the prophecy given through him... becomes a god while still moving about in the flesh.'
St Athanasius wrote that 'God became man so that we might become deified.'
St Cyril of Alexandria said that we 'are called "temples of God" and indeed "gods," and so we are.'

St Basil the Great stated that 'becoming a god' is the highest goal of all.

St Gregory of Nazianzus said, 'become gods for (God's) sake, since (God) became man for our sake.'

Even the Bible says we are gods. In Psalm 82, which is then quoted by Jesus himself, we are told that we are gods (Psalm 82:6, John 10:34). Surely that needs some understanding in the context of Jesus claiming to be the Son of God in John 10:36? What did he mean? Are we all like he was, but just in the caterpillar stage, undeveloped? Can we fly?

'Why change?' some may say. Why should we mess with two thousand-year-old expressions of faith? The simple answer is because we have progressed and change is inevitable. The only sure thing in life is change. In the last five hundred years, we have developed a whole other language to describe both the world in which we live, and our physiological, psychological and spiritual composition. We understand so much more about the universe, science and our physiological and psychological makeup, that many of the old ways of understanding no longer fit the purpose. And the purpose is to help us to awaken to the reality of the spiritual path we are all on, whether we know it or not. But where do we start?

What about the Bible?

A good place to start changing our perspective is the foundational document of Christianity – the Bible, the Holy Scriptures. This is a collection of documents of totally different styles and genres, written by different people at different times, for different reasons. The Old Testament is often referred to now as the Hebrew Scriptures, as this was and still is the Jewish holy writings. Some of the writing we can say is inspired, but some is not. For example, how can it be the word of a compassionate God to command genocide and ethnic cleansing as we see in the story of Joshua?

> So Joshua defeated the whole land, the hill country and the Negeb and the lowland and the slopes, and all their kings; he left no one remaining, but utterly destroyed all that breathed, *as the LORD God of Israel commanded.* (Joshua 10:40)

What kind of a God is that to reverence and worship? Whoever wrote the Book of Joshua were men (and they were *men*) of their time. Scholars tell us that it was written whilst the Israelites were in captivity in Babylon, to encourage them and remind them of their importance and their heritage. It was, in other words, pure spin, based on the oral stories handed down, written to give a despairing people some hope! There's nothing wrong with that, it was a good motive. But instead of regarding the Bible as the infallible, inerrant word of God, we can look at it as a variety of historical texts written in a patriarchal society by men (yes, again, *men!*) some of whom felt inspired by what they believed to be divine revelation, and who sought and struggled to interpret what they had received or discovered, often to encourage and embolden their people. We should ask an important question of these writings: are they *life-affirming* or *life-denying*? Just because something *appears* to come to us from a transcendent source, it does not necessarily follow that it is good. As we know, many atrocities have been committed by individuals who claimed to be guided by God. Terrorist bombers make the same claim. We are an easily deluded people.

This whole subject will be looked at in more detail in Book 2, as it is so crucial to gain an understanding of sacred texts that do not drift into places of denial of common sense and wisdom.

What about Church Teaching?

There are beliefs and doctrines in mainstream Christianity that we no longer find to be life-affirming. The idea of original sin has been seriously challenged by the more affirmative idea of original blessing. God blesses his creation numerous times in Genesis 1. Did we forget that? Also, there are ways of interpreting the life and death of Jesus of Nazareth that we no longer find to be helpful to the human spirit, and the well-being of the planet as a whole. Was God really punishing Jesus for our sin? Or is that a distortion of a deeper truth? How did we get to this situation? What was the process of the development of Christianity as it has been handed down to us?

It obviously all started with the Jesus event, the person of Jesus of Nazareth. But the only accounts we have of his life are in gospel texts written 40–70 years after his death. These were hugely influenced by the Hebrew Scriptures that were written down 100–600 years *before* his life. In fact you could say the gospel writers raided the Hebrew Scriptures to fill out the account of his life and make it fit in with their thought-world of the time.

This sounds a challenging concept in today's world of accuracy versus fake news, but it wasn't seen as unusual or deceitful at the time. It was normal to give a gloss, a spin to life stories. Writers often put in some miraculous events around the birth of a famous person to give a boost to what they were going to say about their life. It basically said to the reader 'Listen up! This is what happened at this person's birth – now hear what a great man he was!' The stories around Jesus' birth have a lot in common with Greek and Roman stories around the birth of famous men of old, many of whom were contemporary with Jesus. They are *not* unusual. The birth of Emperor Augustus was foretold by portents of a miraculous star, according to Roman historian Suetonius. He also describes a similar story to Herod's slaughter of the innocents, as Roman leaders were told that no male child should be reared. Virgil wrote that Romulus and Remus were conceived by divine impregnation by the god Mars. Alexander the Great's father was sent a dream that the child would be conceived from a divine source and he should not sleep with his wife. And so on...

* * *

In addition to understanding writing conventions of the time, we have to realise that the four Gospels writers were influenced by the earlier writers of the letters that are in the New Testament. All of Paul's letters were written before any of the gospels, so the concepts and ideas he developed were to some extent fleshed out in the gospel stories. Paul was an ex-Pharisee, steeped in the Hebrew Scriptures and with a turn of mind that was mystically inspired at times, analytical sometimes, controlling at others, and downright confusing on occasion.

Later came the early theologians of the church, who gradually decided, according to their own wisdom and insight at the time, what should be included in both scripture and doctrine, and, more pointedly, what should be eradicated as 'heresy'. Much of this process was more politically and power-base inspired than spiritually inspired. Many of the so-called heresies were 'lost Christianities', ways of thinking that had flourished in the first 200–300 years of Christianity. The word 'heresy' comes from the Greek word *hairesis* which means 'choice'. Early Christians were able to choose which texts they favoured and base their belief on those texts. Some of these texts have recently been rediscovered through research and archaeological finds such as the Nag Hammadi scrolls; others have continued to practise their own forms of Christianity quietly in out-of-the-way places.

Gradually, over the first 1000 years, the Christian Church fossilised into an unchallengeable body of doctrine and dogma. It was a long process. To challenge it meant accusations of blasphemy and heresy, and death by various unpleasant means, burnings, beheadings and other tortures. All of which was a long way from the call of the founder to 'love your neighbour as yourself.' For Christianity to be believable within our present-day understanding of the universe and our relationships with all other beings, we have to look afresh at many of our inherited Christian doctrines. Christianity has to expand to reach the fulfilment of its founder's intention.

Some of the Questions to Be Asked

1. What concepts has Christianity gathered that are not helpful and life-affirming?

Here are some examples that I feel need to be revisited:

- Jesus as the *only-begotten Son* of God. What does that really mean? How are Jesus and the Cosmic, Universal Christ to be interpreted? There is a deeper meaning within the wisdom teaching, which we shall come to.
- The inheritance of the idea from temple worship that God demands a physical sacrifice. That's not what many of the later prophets of the Hebrew scriptures said. Have a look at Hosea 6:6, or Amos 5:20–24, or Micah 6:6–8. They express the idea that God doesn't want all that blood and sacrifice, he just wants humanity to 'do justice, love kindness and walk humbly with God.' It's quite simple really!
- The wrath of God. Does the Divine Source really get angry, or is that just our way of thinking? Humans get very angry, therefore did past writers assumed God must be like that as well? Was it a way of interpreting the sufferings of life in those times?
- Salvation: is it a promise for the future or a path of wholeness and healing for right now? What about sanctification? Is that the same thing?
- God is not male! The Bible was written in an era of male patriarchy and the language derived from it. It has to be challenged and changed. God is beyond gender, but our language is limited.

19

- Interpreting the Bible stories. Creation? The Tower of Babel? Noah's Ark? The Nativity? How do we interpret these ancient stories for today? The nativity story is still often seen as literal, instead of metaphorical. Once we understand why the writers created these stories, we can see them for the symbolic creations they are.

2. What omissions are there?

What has been squashed or eradicated in the process of creating the Church? For example:

- Jesus as a wisdom teacher of the path of transformation. The wisdom path has a long lineage both within Christianity and in other indigenous and mystery traditions.
- The lost Christianities that were gradually quashed in the third and fourth centuries as the bishops sought to impose order and the Romans institutionalised the faith. Rediscovery of various ancient texts has shed light on other versions of the faith.
- The other scriptures that were left out of the canon of the New Testament, such as the recently rediscovered Gospels of Thomas, Philip and Mary Magdalene.
- The lost doctrine of reincarnation or rebirth, which was never truly banned in Church doctrine. The Bible does not rule it out, it simply doesn't address the issue.

3. What needs to be added from our current understanding? For example:

- New insights from areas of science, sociology and systems theory, such as deep ecology, evolution of consciousness, quantum physics insights, epigenetics, psychology, psychoneuroimmunology, the concept of a holographic universe, energy and information fields, etc.

- Insights from other faiths, including from the so-called 'new age' teachings, some of which actually incorporate the ageless wisdom teaching newly rediscovered.
- Complementary healing techniques and therapies, whose beneficial effects are increasingly being recognised.
- Prayer, intention and meditation – much scientific research has been done into understanding the efficacy and benefits of these spiritual practices.

I hope to address all these issues and more in the Wisdom Series of several books, including questions for reflection, practices for your own spiritual development, and signposts for further study.

Questions for Reflection

1. Think of some ways that traditional Christian teaching helps you? Make a note of them and take them into a time of prayer and reflection. In what ways have they helped?
2. What do you find unhelpful about traditional Christianity? What emotions do they bring up in you? What do you disagree with? How have you handled that disagreement?
3. How have your views changed over the years? Think back to the early days of your spiritual path. What has evolved in your way of thinking about it?

Practice

Try using this version of the Lord's Prayer as a daily practice for a week or so. What effect does it have on you, compared to the traditional version?

O Breath of Life, flowing in all creation,
    may the light of your presence fill the universe.
Your way of being come, your desire be done,

in this and all realms of existence.

Bring forth the nourishment and insight we need for this day.

May forgiveness of self and others be our lived reality.

Liberate us from all things that bind us and deliver us from unhealthiness.

For you are abundant life, creative unity and glorious harmony,

through all time and beyond. Amen.

[The Lord's Prayer, based on translations from Aramaic by Neil Douglas-Klotz]

Signposts for Further Study
Books

Bourgeault, Cynthia, 2008. *The Wisdom Jesus: Transforming Heart and Mind – a New Perspective on Christ and His Message.* Boston: Shambhala Publications Inc.

Borg, Marcus, 2003. *The Heart of Christianity.* New York: HarperCollins

Henson, John, 2010. *Wide Awake Worship: Hymns and Prayers Renewed for the 21st Century.* Winchester UK: O Books

Ehrman, B. D., 2003. *Lost Christianities: The Battles for Scripture and the Faiths We Never Knew.* New York: Oxford University Press

Smith, Adrian B., 2005. *Tomorrow's Christian: A New Framework for Christian Living.* Winchester UK: O Books

Treston, Kevin, 2018. *The Wind Blows Where it Chooses: The Quest for a Christian Story for our Time.* Bayswater, Australia: Coventry Press

Schwatzentruber, Michael (ed.), 2006. *The Emerging Christian Way.* Kelowna, Canada: CopperHouse

Websites

CANA: Awakening to Universal Spirituality: Evolving with

Christianity – www.cana.org.uk

Progressive Christianity Network Britain: www.pcnbritain. org.uk/

Progressive Christianity USA: progressivechristianity.org/

Modern Church, an international society promoting liberal Christian theology, working ecumenically to encourage open, enquiring, non-dogmatic approaches to Christianity. modernchurch.org.uk/

Living Spirituality Connections, a hub for creative ways of exploring spirituality. It is at the interface between traditional Christian faith and practice and newly emerging expressions of spirituality. www.livingspirit.org.uk/

One Spirit Alliance, networking to promote and provide a forum for spiritually-minded people and organisations to foster connection and collaboration between them. onespiritalliance.net/

Chapter 2

Change Is All Around Us

To improve is to change; to be perfect is to change often.
John Henry Newman

Change will not come if we wait for some other person or
some other time. We are the ones we've been waiting for. We
are the change that we seek.
Barack Obama

If you change the way you look at things, the things you look
at change.
Wayne Dyer

I've changed. In my teens and early twenties, I was agnostic,
arrogant, self-centred. In my late twenties and early thirties I
was seeking meaning for existence. In my late thirties I was a
card-carrying evangelical charismatic Christian. And as time
has gone on, I have broadened, deepened and expanded in my
beliefs and hopefully become a better person for it. Change is
inevitable in the journey of life. We evolve.

Looking back in time at how evolution has occurred, we can
see that there have been certain changes, certain evolutionary
leaps in relationship between separate parts that have resulted
in huge steps forward:

- When atoms first started joining together to make
  molecules.
- When complex organic molecules began to form into such
  complex structures that they became self-regulating and
  life began as science defines it.

- When the first basic cells developed a relationship with the chemical chlorophyll and could harness the energy of the sun to make oxygen that has filled our atmosphere.
- When sea creatures found how to breathe in the oxygen and live on land.

And on and on, the march of evolution as things come into ever more complex relationships.

Eventually, Homo sapiens evolved and at some stage in our evolution speech became possible. This was a big change. Physiologically, in a child's first year its speech is restricted and the sounds it makes are a bit like those of a baby primate, a chimpanzee or whatever. But during the second year, the larynx moves to a lower position, carrying the base of the tongue with it, and the child can make a much wider range of sounds. Speech becomes possible.

This development marked a huge leap in communication for the human race, enabling information to be passed on in detail, and cognitive thought to be developed. But it happened slowly. Eventually, writing developed: a means of recording and sharing information. But manuscripts had to be laboriously written out by hand – until the Gutenberg printing press was invented in the fifteenth century. Over the next half century, eight million books were produced, the philosophy of the ancient world became known, the Bible and other sacred texts became widely accessible, and 'how-to' books on all sorts of skills and crafts became available. Information spread and people learnt.

Soon, this information explosion speeded up. In the 1830s, the telegraph was invented – the written word could be sent across vast distances. Fifty years later, the telephone arrived. Then the wireless radio. Then television, tape recorders, photocopiers – each one amplifying our ability to circulate information. Now we have quantum computers, a technological revolution and the Internet explosion, with more information available than any human brain could possibly ever hold. Yet we can hold it in our hand with a smartphone!

In our own lifetimes, change is happening at an ever-increasing rate, and in every field of human endeavour – technology, marketing, genetics, sporting achievements, psychology, healthcare. It has to happen in spiritual belief as well. Rapid change is upon us, the evolution of the human world. But evolution in human *behaviour* is much slower. One social commentator, Peter Russell, puts it like this in his book, *Waking Up in Time* (p. 38):

> Our power to change the world may have made prodigious leaps, but our internal development, the development of our attitudes and values, has progressed much more slowly. We seem to be as prone to greed, aggression, short-sightedness and self-centredness as we were 2500 years ago... If we are to continue our evolutionary journey, it is imperative that we now make some equally prodigious leaps in our ability to transform our minds... This is the challenge of our times.

Our greatest challenge now is for the level of human consciousness to rise above the tribal thinking that has plagued human society for so long. The level of thinking and behaviour of humanity has to change. Jesus exemplified the change, so long ago, with his transformational teaching to love one another, but it is only now that we have reached the stage of evolution of the mind and consciousness that we can begin to put that into practice on a global level.

Escaping Tribal Thinking

Jesus did not come to change the mind of God about humanity, Jesus came to change the mind of humanity about God. God has no favourites, no preferred privileged people, no in-crowd. God-in-Jesus was trying to move people beyond tribalism.

Tribal thinking deals with opposites. It's what Richard Rohr, in his American drawl, calls 'Stinkin' Thinkin''! In Jesus' time, Judaism decided who it was okay to touch and who was to be rejected, who was to be loved and who was to be hated, who was in the tribe and who was outside. Jesus tried to move us on. Not just to 'love your neighbour', but going further to 'love your enemy'. This is a huge challenge in today's world, as we come face-to-face with fanatical extremism, as we have seen in the senseless, barbaric terrorism that has happened around the globe in recent years. The motive behind the terrorist mentality is tribal thinking at its most extreme – if they are not in our tribe, we will eliminate them. If they don't follow our rules, kill them. As I mentioned in the last chapter, it is actually there in the Bible as well – when Joshua took the Israelites into Canaan, they killed the other tribes, supposedly 'in the name of the Lord'. Let's name it for what it was – it was genocide. Except it wasn't God that was behind it, but humanity's distorted concepts of God. But what the Israelites did 3000 years ago was understandable in the culture and context of the day. Not so ISIS fanatics and their brutal, egocentric, tribal thinking. It's an anathema to the more evolved world.

Jesus challenged tribal thinking that saw some people as 'okay' and others as 'not okay', and eliminated the idea that some people are 'not okay'. He was seeking to re-establish in Judaism the teaching to love, bringing in a new economy of grace and love, which is the very heart of the gospel revolution. He went out of his way to associate with and accept those who were seen as outcasts and sinners – the lepers, the Samaritan woman, the sharp businessmen. Jesus was meant to be a game changer for the human psyche and for religion itself. But to this day we fall back into tribal thinking, rather than focussing on the higher way, on love. Even the very religion founded in the name of Christ fell straight back into tribalism. It became exclusive, defining who was in and who was out. Those who fell into the category of 'out' were going to hell. Tribal thinking also cultivates revenge. Martin Luther King said it:

> Returning hate for hate multiplies hate, adding deeper darkness to a night already devoid of stars. Darkness cannot drive out darkness; only light can do that. Hate cannot drive out hate, only love can do that.

In order for the world to change, the consciousness of humanity has to change. And it is gradually changing, over the generations. One thousand years ago, many Christians had much the same attitude as today's hate-filled terrorists. It led to the crusades. Even during and after the reformation we still had the persecution of anyone who saw things differently, with torture, hangings, decapitations and burning at the stake. Blasphemy and heresy were the tribal ways of identifying those who were outside the tribe and were to be disposed of.

It has taken a long time, but we are gradually becoming more compassionate, more aware, and more able to see all other people as part of the same human race. So we will not and cannot accept the way of seeing the world that terrorist fanatics adopt. We have to resist the evil of fundamentalist terrorism, and it is an international challenge as to how to do this, but we must not seek revenge on these deluded people. For that is what they are, deluded, entering in to a delusion that says their God is right and wants them to kill the infidel. That is not a concept of God that the vast majority of Muslims or people of any religion would ever endorse. The saddest thing of this terrorist regime is that this distorted, barbaric, power-crazed way of thinking has become attached to a religious belief. We have to find a better way.

Jesus also challenged the attitudes we have. He was trying to get us to internalise the values that promote good will and right relationships. It was simple teaching.

- Sort out your anger without taking it out on others (Matthew 5:21–2).
- If you have a disagreement, make it right (Matthew 5:23–6).
- Return kindness for insults, don't retaliate (Matthew 5:38–42).
- Desire the best for others, even if you don't get on (Matthew 5:43–7).

Always forgive, don't judge others, do to them as you would have them do to you, and many other simple, profound teachings that provide the framework for building a healthy, harmonious community. Those are the teachings needed in the world as much now as ever and we each need to embody them, live them out. We need to walk the talk.

A Network of Goodwill

I came across something a few years ago that I thought captured the whole idea of the global shift going on, the change in consciousness of humanity. It was entitled 'A Network of Goodwill' in a little newsletter about inspiring events in North Wales.

In every neighbourhood, there are people who share a vision of a whole and humane world, and who share a commitment to make this vision a reality. Most will have a spiritual discipline, demonstrating that harmony and well-being are initially states of mind and heart. They may practise meditation or mindfulness, and use the insights and strength from their inner work to inform their service in the world.

It went on to mention those who are working to help the planet via environmental concerns, recycling, transition to less oil dependency, and those who are working creatively to restore the soul in arts and music, or in education or community. It also mentioned those working for the healing of both individuals and communities, and those involved in the political arena. It concluded:

> Most are spiritually active, but usually without a conventional creed. Most sense that the world will need a vast outpouring of goodwill if it is to make it through the next few decades intact. Some have found their deeper purpose through personal crisis – perhaps global crisis is humanity's greatest opportunity?

Global Shift

That seems to me to capture the evolution of consciousness that is going on – it's not just happening in one area, one sphere of activity, one group. It's happening globally *and* locally, in all areas of human experience – and thanks to the technological revolution it's all interconnected.

It's a **global shift.** All the established economic, political, cultural and religious institutions of our planet seem to be experiencing increasing change and upheaval, as humanity moves towards the next stage in its evolutionary history. It's happening on all sorts of levels. It's sometimes called the 'Great Awakening' or the 'Great Turning' or 'Earth Awareness' – meaning a change in the way we are approaching life on this planet. It's the transition to a global society in harmony with all Life. We can see the early signs of this emergence everywhere. People are waking up to the change that has to happen. Global warming and climate change has been the trigger for us to awaken. Yes, the world situation looks bleak at times, and many still live in denial that anything can be done. But the changes are already happening. There are new ways of seeing everything:

- New ways of perceiving the world and the nature of

reality, a coming together of science and spirituality. New science tells us that we are all fields of swirling, entangled energetic pulses, interconnected in ways we never dreamt of fifty years ago, undergirded by patterned information fields.

- Flowing from the new science, there are new ways of seeing ourselves as individuals and the nature of humanity as one interconnected whole, with major consequences for how we treat one other and the planet we live in. We are all One.
- There are new practices and actions we can take to heal ourselves and help the planet – increasingly being proven to be effective by science, and therefore gaining in credibility.
- New economics, new politics, new measures of well-being, new global ecological perspectives – it's all bubbling up!

This change in consciousness seems to be happening in the minds and hearts of people throughout the world. The way we have developed the world is failing us – we must find a better way, away from competition and towards cooperation.

We have created the world of today as a result of our collective consciousness, and if we want a better world, each of us has to contribute to the change. We have made the world what it is, and part of that has been through the exclusive nature of Christianity and the thinking that says it is the *only* way, and if you are not in, then you are out and going to hell. That is very close to the ISIS ideology that caused so much suffering in Iraq and Syria in recent years. Only one step further and it becomes 'because you are "out", your life is worthless and of no value.'

Postmodernism and a Different Mindset
Postmodernism is a term which emerged in the 1990s to express a new way of looking at the world. It has been subtly pervasive

in the last 30 years. We can pick out some of its features, although most have a slightly negative feel to them.

- All is relative – there are no absolutes. Context and culture are what determine the truth or 'rightness' of an issue, rather than any appeal to ultimate standards of morality and ethics.
- Authorities and institutions have no right to power. There is a profound distrust of authority figures and a deep cynicism about institutions: the law, the monarchy, the church, the government, the police, the health system, multinational industry and education. They are all 'suspect'. This has given rise to the growth in 'conspiracy theories' with the mindset that no institution is to be trusted.
- Past, respected, familiar traditions are scorned, whilst the future is devoid of hope. Therefore the only thing that matters is living for now. Immediacy becomes the order of the day, instant individual gratification is expected and demanded, and the consumer rules. Look after number one. This goes hand-in-hand with the rise of the drug culture – instant gratification and avoidance of hard reality in one easy dose.
- Audio-visual is the favoured mode of communication, not the written word. It is a video culture, not a book culture, and information is communicated in emotive rather than rational terms, preferably by slogans and soundbites. And now 'Fake News'!
- Rational thought isn't important, what matters is how something *feels*. Why not harbour eight incompatible ideas at the same time? Contradictions are only valid in a world governed by overarching big stories, like Christianity, and those are now suspect and discredited.

That's the way of thinking that crept in during the turn of the century. It has since been modified by the pressing issues of global warming, ecological crisis and the rise of various fundamentalisms and increasing terrorism. In mainstream media, the future is painted as bleak, austere and joyless.

Postmodernism and Religion

Let's face it; postmodern thinking and hierarchical religion do not sit easily together. Old-time religion is 'out', spirituality is 'in'. Belonging to an institution like the Church has little appeal. It has become relegated to just one within a whole host of consumer choices. We live in a 'pick and mix' world. In many ways, Christianity has become a neatly packaged consumer item, sitting on a shelf which is full of other things that we can do with our time.

It's not that the Church has gone over to Mammon, it is simply that the commercial world has latched on to Sundays as another day of the week in which money can be generated. In doing so, it has relegated the church so that it competes with a whole range of leisure pursuits which have the force of modern marketing techniques and financial muscle behind them. It also competes with the pressure of children who want to play football, rugby, go swimming or go to dance classes. Choice and shopping now reign supreme on a Sunday, and the question confronting the Church is how to react and change to communicate the good news in this consumeristic mélange of choice. It's moved from being a faith system that influenced public opinion and determined political policy, to being seen as a minority leisure pursuit. And just what is the good news in this postmodern world?

How can Christianity change and adapt to this new mindset? Something it surely has to think about is styles and times of services of worship. Is Sunday sacrosanct for services? Serried ranks of pews and a didactic sermon is not engaging many. We are in the audio-visual age and virtual church is already with us!

But more importantly, to my mind, is that we have to update our outmoded ways of thinking about the spiritual path. It has to fit today's world and speak into the ecological crisis, the injustices and inequalities, and the lack of compassion and goodwill in society today. It needs a bigger framework in which to sit.

We Are All One

Jesus taught the same universal teaching as is present in all good spiritual paths – to love your neighbour as yourself and to do unto others as you would have them do to you. He also said, 'May they be one, as we are one, I in them and you in me, that they may become completely one' (John 17:22–23). This teaching has now come of age.

The cutting edge of modern science is telling us that we are all interconnected, swirling patterns of energy, and that the same patterns of information are repeated at all levels of being. The emerging view is that the whole of material reality emerges from this vast informational domain which undergirds matter. This is presenting us with new ways of seeing the world – from quantum physics we learn that consciousness is the first cause, the prime mover in the universe, and that at the fundamental level we are all interconnected in an intricate matrix of energy. We are all One. There is one consciousness of which we are each an individualised being. Consciousness itself is described as the Ground of Being, which has also been used as a Christian term for God.

From biology and the new science of epigenetics we learn that our thoughts, intentions and feelings affect our genes, and thus our health. We can gain a much deeper understanding of the power of intention, of prayer, healing and all the spiritual disciplines and therapies – and the positive effects they have on health and length of life. We are becoming much more aware of the potential of the human being for health, healing and wholeness.

And the whole idea of information fields and morphic resonance tells us that any new developments by individuals contribute to the whole collective consciousness of humanity. We can begin to see that what we do as *human beings* makes it easier for other humans to do the same – and the more we do it, the easier it becomes. It gets built in to our collective consciousness, our morphic field. So behaving with compassion, goodwill, kindness, meditating, calling down spiritual energies of love, seeking freedom for the oppressed – when the ball starts rolling, it gathers speed, and brings change. That change is happening now. We are evolving rapidly to a better way of being. It *is* a global shift.

Integrating Worlds

All these developments give us insights into the nature of reality today, and to my mind, they have to be integrated into our Christian understanding of the world. We cannot go through life believing one worldview on Sundays and then living another completely separate worldview the rest of the week. If we live like that we essentially have a duality within us that leads to tension and stress and illness.

Humanity is evolving in its level of consciousness. We are no longer able to accept living with the injustices and inequalities of the world, or with abusive power relationships, or with the polluting nature of our societies. It is no longer okay for us to ignore the plight of people in other parts of the world. We all want to see change, progress, more compassionate responses from world governments, acceptance of indigenous healing traditions, more harmony and goodwill in relationships, more sustainable and environmentally friendly solutions. These are all the teachings of healthy spiritual traditions, not just Christianity. Five hundred years ago, the Spanish Inquisition was burning so-called heretics at the stake. In Britain, the last execution by beheading was in 1747, and the last horrific punishment of being hanged, drawn and quartered took place in 1782. The last death sentence by hanging in Britain was in 1964. Humanity is growing in consciousness, and behind it is the Divine Will-to-Good as a driving force, expressed in love and the gradual betterment of human society. Yes, there are setbacks, but the overall trend is progress to a more compassionate future. This is the shift happening in the world now.

Questions for Reflection

1. How have your perceptions of the world shifted over your lifetime?
2. What has been your gut response to terrorist atrocities? How has that changed over time?
3. What signs of a global shift have you noticed? What is changing?
4. How can we get more positive, constructive news into the mainstream media to counter the sensationalist fear-mongering and tribal thinking?

Practice: Loving-Kindness

The practice of loving-kindness is a wonderful way to grow compassion for yourself and for others. Loving-kindness is unconditional, inclusive love, a love with wisdom. It does not depend on whether one 'deserves' it or not; it is not restricted to those who are close to us; it extends to include all living beings. It applies to ourselves as well. There are no expectations of anything in return. This is the ideal, pure love, which everyone has in potential. We begin with loving ourselves, for unless we have a measure of this unconditional love and acceptance for ourselves, it is difficult to extend it to others. Then we include others who are special to us, and, ultimately, all living things. Gradually, both the visualization and the meditation phrases blend into the actual experience, the feeling of loving kindness.

If we choose deliberately to practise loving kindness in our daily routines, we will become more loving. If we don't, we won't! Here is a practice for growing loving kindness. Set aside a quiet period to go through these simple steps with intention and openness.

1. There is a place of loving kindness inside yourself. Recognise it, honour it, awaken it, and enter it. Show it to yourself.
2. Drawing upon that source of loving kindness within, bring to mind someone close to you whom you love very much. From your source, send loving kindness toward this person and bless them.
3. Now think of someone who is a casual friend or associate – someone not in your inner circle, but a bit further removed, someone you admire or appreciate. Send love to that individual.
4. Now send loving kindness to someone about whom you feel neutral or indifferent – for example, a shop assistant or neighbour. Send your blessing to this person.
5. A little harder now – think of someone who has hurt you, who has talked evil of you, whom you find it difficult to like or you don't enjoy being around. Send this person your love, asking for the best for them.
6. Bring all these people into the stream of flowing love, including yourself. Hold them here for a few moments.
7. Finally, extend this love to embrace all beings in the universe. It is one love towards all, regardless of religion, race, culture, or likability.

Loving kindness will grow with use. You are simply an instrument, a conduit for the inflow and outflow divine energies. Monitor your mind. Be aware of your thinking patterns. Once you are aware of them, you can change them.

Signposts for Further Study
Books

Russell, Peter, 2009. *Waking Up in Time.* Llandeilo: Cygnus Books

Tacey, David, 2004. *The Spirituality Revolution: the emergence of contemporary spirituality.* Hove UK: Brunner-Routledge

Schacker, Michael, 2013. *Global Awakening: New Science and 21st-Century Enlightenment.* Rochester VT: Park Street Press

Websites

The Shift Network – a transformative education company that partners with teachers, experts, and healers on the planet, across many diverse fields, to offer experiences that support your growth and transformation, to create a better world. theshiftnetwork.com/

Chapter 3

The Evolving Scientific Worldview

Before I was a vicar, I was a science teacher, and bringing those two sides of my life together has always been part of my spiritual path. I've taught many school students the simple version of the nature of matter, each atom being made up of a nucleus with electrons whizzing around it in orbit. I've taught about electricity being a movement of free electrons in metal. Neither of these are strictly true. At the same time, I was aware of a deeper level of elementary particles that were being discovered, the gluons, muons, bosons and quarks, and that in reality everything was tiny vortices of energy.

Nothing is actually solid, it is really interlaced patterns of energy, creating force fields that give us the feeling of different textures to our sense of touch. It is our eyes that receive the reflected light from these force fields and send the information to the brain, which then makes sense of it all. And so, a table is pictured in our minds as something brown and made of wood, not just an incredibly complicated interlacing of energies and forces held in a pattern that came from the pattern for an oak tree. We don't see the forces and energies holding the table in shape, we just see the shape. This is what our consciousness does in the brain, its receptor and filter mechanism. This is a huge leap for most people to take on board, that reality as we see it is not how it actually is at all. It's as much of a shift for many scientists as it is for us ordinary folks. It actually became easier for me to understand it all as I gained a deeper understanding of theology and perennial wisdom. I could see that there was an underlying information pattern, a Divine Matrix, which held everything in being. Science is beginning to think along the same lines.

Many scientists are still stuck in an old way of thinking. The scientific paradigm is beginning at last to shift from a totally materialistic scientism to the realisation that the weight of evidence is pointing to consciousness as the prime mover. In science, there are three particular areas of shift that interest me, and I want to briefly mention each of them: Consciousness, Epigenetics, and Information Fields.

The Hard Problem of Consciousness

Human consciousness, that part of us that makes us aware of ourselves, seems to be growing, changing, and evolving. But it is a slippery concept for scientists. The famous physicist, Sir Roger Penrose said,

> My position on consciousness demands a major revolution in physics... I've come to believe that there is something very fundamental missing from current science... Our understanding at this time is not adequate and we're going to have to move to new regions of science.

Many other physicists find consciousness an intractable problem. Edward Witten is a professor of mathematical physics at the Institute for Advanced Study, Princeton, New Jersey. In 2004, Time magazine stated that Witten is widely thought to be the world's smartest living theoretical physicist. He said,

> I have a much easier time imagining how we would understand the Big Bang, even though we can't do it yet, than I can imagine understanding consciousness.

The Nobel-prize winning quantum physicist, Erwin Schrödinger also has views on the fundamental nature of consciousness. He said,

> Consciousness cannot be accounted for in physical terms.

For consciousness is absolutely fundamental. It cannot be accounted for in terms of anything else.

So scientific research has made little progress with consciousness, even though it has been trying for many years. Basically, scientists can't get a hold on consciousness, it's as if it exists outside of the known laws of the universe and reality as we know it – and maybe it does. There seems to be a growing awareness that human consciousness may have to be regarded as a 'given' in nature, not something that can be proved or disproved, but which just *is*. We know we have it, but we can't define it, dismantle it, separate it, or see what it is made of. How very frustrating for the scientific mind! How very mystifying!

Consciousness and quantum physics are connected. A basic insight, from the quantum theory of the 1920s, is that particles are formed when the wave of potential is collapsed by the act of being observed. Observation is an act of consciousness. In other words, consciousness has to exist before any material particles can. We perceive things into existence! It's taken ninety years for it to percolate down from academia to you and me. This has birthed an area of huge contention amongst physicists and highlights the tension between those who stick with existing scientific materialism and those who are more free thinking and willing to embrace new concepts that challenge the old. The materialists firmly believe that everything in the universe is derived from physical matter. To them, consciousness *has to* have emerged from the neural interconnections in the brain. No other consideration is possible. But to the more free-thinking physicists, the physical world exists within consciousness, from which everything emerges. They just don't yet have a theory for what consciousness is! This is not unusual. Physicists now believe that 95% of the universe is made up of dark matter and dark energy – but they have no working theory as to what that is!

The new belief is that consciousness is fundamental in the universe, not derived from physical matter. Matter comes from Mind, not Mind from Matter! We are all a part of that consciousness, all emanating from it. Consciousness holds everything in being, and this consciousness works through energy fields. Everything consists of energy fields, not matter. Matter is 'frozen energy'. It basically says that consciousness is not a phenomenon of the brain, but is a kind of huge matrix, the ground of being, in which all material possibilities are held in potential and from which all material reality has emerged. In this model, the human brain acts as receiver which filters a tiny trickle of this vast consciousness. This tiny trickle is what gives us our notion of 'self' and our perception of reality.

Informational Domains

An even more recently emerging scientific worldview says that beyond energy, there is an informational domain out of which all reality is derived. The entire universe is a projection emanating from that informational domain. Informational patterns are repeated at all levels. There is an intrinsic simplicity and innate wholeness to our Universe. The same patterns are found in a variety of natural phenomena. For instance, fractals are the pattern that can be seen in the irregularity of a coastline, in snowflakes, in the complexity of entire weather systems, in the corrosion patterns of metals, in the crystalline structures of super conductors, in the solar wind and in the structure of Saturn's rings. Even galaxies cluster in fractal patterns! Many more examples are given in Dr. Jude Currivan's book, *The Cosmic Hologram*. When seen from that perspective, the universe does behave like a cosmic hologram, with form being brought into being according to the patterns held in the informational domain, guided by consciousness. From the macro to the micro, the same patterns exist, as if the informational domain holds the pattern for everything. Consciousness is what brings reality into being following these informational patterns. From the patterns, consciousness forms energies which in turn bring about physical matter as the quantum energy fields collapse to make particles. Everything participates in this; everything has some level of consciousness which contributes to the whole. Even an atom has its pattern, its right to exist and behave in a certain way.

The concept of a universal consciousness speaks into the whole realm of spirituality, across all religions. The mystical experience of oneness, or unitive consciousness is common to all faiths and spiritual traditions. It is when we are able to put aside or go beyond our own self-centred nature that we can enter into unitive consciousness, oneness with the All. Sometimes that just happens, albeit fleetingly, but the common and unifying factor in spiritual paths that helps us all to awaken is meditation. At the end of this chapter is a simple meditation outline and links to many different organisations advocating Christian forms of meditation and contemplative prayer.

Consciousness Is the Ground of Being.

God as the Ground of Being was a theological description first introduced by the scholar Paul Tillich in the 1950s. It corresponds closely with the idea of consciousness and information as the domain from which everything emanates. But it does give a different picture of God from traditional understanding. It says that everything contains God, everything is part of the divine nature. If we equate God with the consciousness of Being, the exciting thing is that this theology fits very well with the new scientific paradigm. Rather than science disproving religion, it seems that science is on a path of new discovery that will end up proving the reality of the realms of soul and spirit. I believe consciousness is the third force that will marry science and spirituality. Theologically, it is *panentheism*, the theory that everything is within the Divine Source, and the Divine Source is within everything.

Epigenetic Revelations

The second scientific insight is a biological one, drawing on the work of Dr Bruce Lipton. Epigenetics is the study of what goes on *around* the gene. It analyses the way in which genes are activated by the environment in which they exist. Experiments have shown that the DNA helix is surrounded by a sheath of protein molecules that act like switches by unwrapping the genes. But what makes the switches work is the environment surrounding the cell. More precisely, the electro-magnetic and chemical signals in the environment around the cell are what 'flick the switches'. On the surface of every cell are various receptors for chemical and electro-magnetic signals. They work in two ways. Firstly, our own thought processes cause the release of chemicals into the bloodstream. This is happening rapidly, all the time. Genes are being wrapped up and unwrapped constantly as we speak, by our thoughts and emotions and our unconscious body-regulating mechanisms. We are constantly changing our gene expression.

Secondly, the environment around the cell is affected by the electro-magnetic radiation and fields of energy that are given out by all manner of living beings, including ourselves. There are protein receptors on the surface of the cell that register these messages and convey them to the genes. It is these more subtle energies that are suspected to be how one person can influence the well-being of another – by affecting which genes are in operation.

One of the writers in this area, Dawson Church, put it like this in his book, *The Genie in Your Genes*:

When you understand that with every feeling and thought, in every instant, you are performing epigenetic engineering upon your own cells, you suddenly have a degree of leverage over your health and happiness that makes all the difference.

This not only places the responsibility for our health firmly back with each of us, but it also opens up a whole area of understanding about the power of intention, of thinking positive thoughts, of prayer, healing and meditation and all the spiritual disciplines and therapies – and the positive effects they have on health and length of life.

We are becoming much more aware of the potential of the human being for health, healing and wholeness – but it all stems from an evolved understanding of the role that our own consciousness has.

Morphogenetic Fields

The third area of shift is to do with Dr Rupert Sheldrake's theory of morphic resonance, which has been around since the 1980s. His basic idea is that every species has its own morphic field, a sort of collective consciousness that is affected by what members of that species do. So if rats in a lab in New York learn a new behaviour, then that affects the morphic field of rats, and rats in labs in Australia will learn that new behaviour more quickly. Sheldrake has collected a great deal of evidence to back up his theory. Scaling it up to human behaviour, what we do as *human beings* makes it easier for other humans to do the same – and the more we do it, the easier it becomes. So behaving with compassion, meditating, sending the energies of love, seeking freedom for the oppressed – when the ball starts rolling, it gathers speed, and brings change. That change is happening now. We are evolving rapidly to a better way of being. We are undergoing an evolution in consciousness as the human race moves towards a better way of being.

Christianity and Consciousness

Christianity doesn't use consciousness as a theological term. Christianity speaks more of Divine Love and the nature of Christ. But the perennial wisdom tradition does, in that it sees Consciousness as the offspring of Divine Will and Divine Intelligence. Lucille Cedercrans explains this clearly in the first chapter of her book *The Nature of the Soul*. There is One Divine Mind, One Ultimate Life that enlivens all, and this has two aspects, the Father Aspect (Will and Purpose) and the Mother Aspect (Intelligence and Creativity). These two interact to give 'birth' to the third aspect, the Son Aspect, or Loving Consciousness. This does, of course, tie in quite well with the doctrine of the Holy Trinity, if the Holy Spirit can change gender and become the Mother Aspect of the One Life, that female energy that has been sadly lacking in Christianity since its birth. The Roman Catholic Church tried to fill the gaping hole with notions of the Blessed Virgin Mary being the Queen of Heaven, but the root of the problem lay in the earlier definition of the Trinity, it being all male.

From this lofty understanding of the nature of the One God, Perennial Wisdom teachings speak of the emanations or rays of God that work through all creation, holding it in being, constantly creating and evolving form in our physical world. These are the blueprints or patterns which science is beginning to speak of in terms of informational domains.

If we look at the beginning of the gospel of John, we find this:

In the beginning was the Word, and the Word was with God, and the Word was God. He was with God in the beginning. Through him all things were made... In him was life, and that life was the light of all mankind. (John 1:1–4)

A word is a pattern of letters and sound. If we substitute 'Pattern' for 'Word', the passage comes close to a statement of the scientific understanding of the informational domains from which everything emerges.

In the beginning was the Pattern, and the Pattern was with

God, and the Pattern was God. It was with God in the beginning. Through it all things were shaped... In it was life, and that life was the light of all beings.

There is a lot of work to be done here in tying together new science, consciousness, quantum physics, patterns of information, and understandings coming from deep religious theology and practices. My previous book, *Blue Sky God* has laid some of the ground work for this, and a future book will go into some greater depth. The problem of language is one to overcome, but I have a strong feeling that the languages of science and spirit are on a convergent course and will each illuminate the other before much longer. Eighty years ago, the author Alice A. Bailey wrote as much in a prophetic paragraph:

We stand expectantly awaiting the dawn of that day when religion will stand upon a scientific basis and the truths to which the ages bear witness will be substantiated and proven... Then there will emerge a new race, with new capacities, new ideals, new concepts about God and matter, about life and spirit. Through the humanity of the future there will be seen... a soul, an entity, who will manifest its own nature, which is love, wisdom and intelligence. (Alice A. Bailey, *The Soul and Its Mechanism*, p. 152)

I haven't touched upon the realm of human experience that flies in the face of the materialist scientific view. Extrasensory perception, remote viewing, telepathy, near-death experiences, telekinesis, auras, etc. are all areas that have been extensively researched, with many peer-reviewed, published papers in all sorts of journals. The efficacy of many healing therapies has been demonstrated without a proven scientific understanding of how they work. These are all areas that can be understood far better with expanded scientific and spiritual viewpoints.

The prevailing materialist scientific worldview still sees them as 'woo-woo' stuff. Yet there is good hard evidence for much of it. Sadly, for many people if something does not fit their worldview they will dismiss it without examination rather than expand their worldview. I am reminded of the second saying in the Gospel of Thomas:

Yeshua says, If you are searching, you must not stop until you find. When you find, however, you will become troubled. Your confusion will give way to wonder.

Many people stop at the 'troubled' point and refuse to go further, turning back to what they already know and accept, thus missing out on awe and wonder!

Questions to Reflect Upon

1. When you find something which doesn't fit with your current understanding, what is your reaction? Do you dismiss it or are you curious to know more?
2. What difference does it make to you to realise that the world is one interconnected whole?
3. Understanding the whole of creation as undergirded by God as the Ground of Being implies that God is within everyone of us. Does that conflict with existing traditional Christian theology for you?

Practice: Meditation

Meditation or contemplative silence is a fundamental part of spiritual practice for transformation. There are different ways, this is one. If you are unfamiliar with it, I invite you to experience it for yourself.

Choose somewhere quiet where you can sit comfortably. Maybe light a candle.

Shut your eyes and relax your body, calm your emotions and

bring your mind to a focus.

Let go of thoughts.

Become aware of the fullness of silence, of God-presence, within and around you. When thoughts pop in, let them go again.

It can help to follow the rhythm of your breath, or to use an anchor – a word or short phrase or to look at the candle flame. Here are some suggestions:

Love

Light

Peace

Be Still

As soon as you realise your mind has wandered, come back to your anchor.

After about five to ten minutes or whenever you are ready, open your eyes.

Give thanks and blow out the candle, sending light and love out into the world.

There are many methods of meditation. Some are rooted in the Christian tradition of contemplative prayer. If you wish to develop this practice, here are two organisations which offer a similar teaching:

The World Community for Christian Meditation

UK: www.christianmeditation.org.uk/

USA: wccm.org/

Contemplative Outreach

UK: contemplativeoutreach.org.uk/

USA: www.contemplativeoutreach.org/

Signposts for Further Study
Books:

Church, Dawson, 2007. *The Genie in your Genes.* Santa Rosa: Elite Books

Currivan, Jude, 2017. *The Cosmic Hologram: In-formation at the Center of Creation*. Rochester VT: Inner Traditions

Lazslo, Erwin, & Dennis, Kingsley (Eds.), 2012. *The New Science and Spirituality Reader*. Rochester VT: Inner Traditions

Lipton, Bruce, 2005. *The Biology of Belief*. Santa Rosa: Elite Books

Mack, John E. & Pfeiffer, Trish (Eds.). *Mind Before Matter: Visions of a New Science of Consciousness*. Winchester UK: O Books

MacGregor, Don, 2012. *Blue Sky God: The Evolution of Science and Christianity*. Winchester UK: Circle Books

Parkinson, Frank, 2009. *Science and Religion at the Crossroads*. Exeter UK: Imprint Academic

Russell, Peter, 2002. *From Science to God: The Mysteries of Consciousness and the Meaning of Light*. Las Vegas: Elf Rock Productions

Websites

Peter Russell has been exploring and writing for many years in the area of science and consciousness and there are many interesting articles on his website: www.peterrussell.com

Rupert Sheldrake, PhD, is a biologist and author best known for his hypothesis of morphic resonance, but also his critique of the distorted methodology of materialist science. www.sheldrake.org/

Bruce Lipton is best known for his ground-breaking work on epigenetics and the power of the subconscious mind. www.brucelipton.com/

Whole World-View: Based on Jude Currivan's book *The Cosmic Hologram*, the scientifically-based WholeWorld-View site reconciles with universal spiritual experiences to co-create a breakthrough in the understanding of the nature of reality, the evolutionary moment we are living in, what it means to be human, and our influence on the evolution of life on our planet. www.wholeworld-view.org/

Chapter 4

Ecological Imperatives

Have you cut yourself recently? Or bought a new pair of shoes that have caused a blister? Or done some damage to your body in some way? After we damage ourselves, healing takes place. With a cut or a burn or a blister, some process we barely understand goes to work to heal the skin. Healing just happens, we don't have to think about it. The pattern that determines the human body is designed to heal itself. Our body takes care of itself.

The same is true of the Earth. There are checks and balances in the natural world – we call them eco-systems. Forces and cycles that work slowly but endlessly to heal the world, bringing it to a place of harmony and interdependency. Poisons get broken down to their harmless constituents in the sea and air. Trees convert the carbon dioxide that humans breathe out into the oxygen that we need. Everything gets deconstructed and recycled in the circle of life. This is the divine pattern for the planet, every part supporting some other part and every creature in its place. There are all manner of cycles that we see at work, endlessly bringing the world back into balance.

But what happens when humans invent chemicals so complex that the sea fights a losing battle to keep pace with the poisons poured into it (poisons such as those we use to varnish our nails or give toilet paper a pretty colour)? Or when humans pull down trees so fast that those left cannot cope with the vast quantities of harmful gas we release so that each of us can be driven around in our own little metal box? What happens when humanity produces a fantastic material that has myriads of helpful uses, but which will not break down for thousands of years and will clog up our seas and land and food chains? What happens when oceans are overfished, when land is polluted, when the ice caps at the poles melt? What are we leaving as an inheritance for our children's children?

These are all big issues, probably the biggest, in the world today. Climate change, global warming, carbon footprint, extinction of species, plastic pollution, animal welfare and agribusiness pollution are all enormous problems to be addressed. Christianity is not a bystander in this. It has been accused of ignoring the plight of the Earth, seeing it as something that could be dominated, stemming from verses in Genesis:

> And God blessed them, and God said unto them, be fruitful, and multiply, and replenish the Earth, and subdue it: and have dominion over the fish of the sea, and over the fowl of the air, and over every living thing that moveth upon the Earth. (Genesis 1:28, KJV)

Well, we have subdued and dominated, violated and polluted to the extent that we face our own extinction if we don't do something about it. The Earth will correct the imbalance, with probably disastrous results for the human race. Part of changing our attitude to our relationship with the planet is a growing change in spiritual approach. Back in the 1960s, Rachel Carson wrote *Silent Spring*, which brought the issue of the indiscriminate use of pesticides to the public attention and helped give birth to the environmental movement (and Joni Mitchell's great song 'Big Yellow Taxi'!). Despite this, we have carried on degrading the biosphere at an ever increasing rate.

In the last forty years, political parties in Europe have seen the need to take on environmentally sound policies. I remember campaigning for the Ecology Party (which became the Green Party) back in the early 1980s, when ideas like developing renewable energy sources, recycling rubbish, growing organic food and putting a tax on polluting cars in cities was seen as wacky, way out stuff. I had a heated discussion with fellow teachers who were all Labour supporters. They thought I was mad to support the Greens, their policies would never happen. Well, it's all happening now! It was staring us in the face back then, but most couldn't see it. As Jesus said, 'Let those who have ears, hear.'

Animal Rights

Increasingly, our consciences are becoming tenderised (pun intended) on the subject of animal welfare. Should live animals be exported for meat? Should geese be force-fed, chickens battery reared or calves given a short life indoors without ever even seeing a green field, in order to provide luxury food for thoughtless gourmets? Should milk production be of such a large scale that cows are kept in barns all year round as milk machines and calves are removed from their mothers within days of birth? It is obviously wrong, but the forces of cheap food production and consumer demand have ridden roughshod over protesting voices, and only now are people beginning to question how their food arrives on their plate. How has that live animal been treated? Does that affect the quality and vibrational energy of the product? Could there be a more compassionate way to farm?

Consumers are now increasingly conscious of their power as a pressure group, and businesses are ever more aware that they must respond to public opinion. Renewable energy schemes are popular with the public, not just for economic reasons, but in order to husband resources and minimise the effect of greenhouse gases upon global warming. The outcry against plastic pollution has reached a crescendo and companies are rushing to implement plans for alternatives to plastic bags and wrappings. There has been a growing public awareness of the need to preserve the viability of the planet. There is also no shortage of doomsday scenarios, for example, the prospect of the majority of the world's seaboard cities being swamped by rising sea levels, or plagues of antibiotic resistant diseases or dust bowls replacing arable land and forests.

But although, years ago, people did protest at losing the habitat of a rare snail when a bypass was planned to relieve a gridlocked Newbury, UK, the road did go ahead. And although we agree that traffic pollution causes asthma and other breathing problems, and maybe contributes to lung cancer and Alzheimer's disease, few of us are prepared to forego the use of private cars. We like the convenience too much. We choose to buy cheap eggs and turn a blind eye to the plight of battery or barn-reared hens. We choose not to look at how an intelligent pig is reared and slaughtered for making bacon. Milk as a staple food within our diet justifies the removal of calves from their mothers. Have you ever heard the outcry from the mothers when their calves are taken? It is pitifully distressing. Even for the well-intentioned, personal choice comes down heavily in favour of cost and convenience over altruism and ethics. The hard fact of it is that humanity is the problem – me, you, our neighbours, the people we work with. It's our attitudes and actions that are causing the despoiling of God's creation.

Part of the Christian heritage takes a decidedly negative path and simply sees us all as 'miserable sinners'. That phrase, from the Book of Common Prayer, was recited every Sunday in the service of Morning Prayer around the world in the Anglican Church *for 400 years*. It was only in the 1960s that different liturgies began to be used. It stems from the doctrine of Original Sin, which was a theology developed out of the story of Adam and Eve and the Fall in Genesis Chapter Three. You know the story – the apple and the serpent, Eve's temptation and Adam's disobedience. It has been an endless source of jokes! But the idea that we can do nothing about our built-in original sin leads to a fatalistic attitude. I can't do it, I will fail, but God forgives me anyway. So, I'll give in to the temptation to buy this cheap bacon, even though I think it's probably been mistreated – I'll just ignore that institutional sin.

To me, Original Sin misses the meaning of the story altogether. Adam and Eve existed in this blissful state with God, until they ate of the tree of knowledge of good and evil – then they became aware they were naked and put on the fig-leaves and hid from God, and were cast out of the Garden of Eden. That speaks to me of a time in human evolution when our brains developed to the stage where we became self-aware, we began to see ourselves in a different light, we became self-conscious. At that stage we became aware of ourselves as individuals, separate from God, no longer held in a blissful state of innocence. As the individuality took hold, so our egos started to develop – we became self-aware, but the cost was that we began to lose our awareness of being one with the divine. Ego, necessary for our development and growth in consciousness, gave rise to wanting things for ourselves, to desire, to greed, to envy, and the roots of all that is wrong with our world. The spiritual journey is about finding our way back into the presence of God, back to Eden. But it only happens as we rise above our lower, self-centred nature and begin to be centred in a higher, more compassionate godly nature.

This is the meaning of some of the enigmatic phrases Jesus said:

> Then Jesus told his disciples, 'If any want to become my followers, let them deny themselves and take up their cross and follow me.' (Matthew 16:24)

Denying ourselves is about *not paying attention* to the ego, the lower desire-nature, the part of self which is our experience of separateness from God. Denying the ego is hard, it is a cross to bear, a cross to be picked up. So Jesus was saying lay down your ego and pick up the cross of surrender and follow me, live like I do.

Those who find their life will lose it, and those who lose their life for my sake will find it. (Matthew 10:39)

On the surface, that makes little sense. But what if we rephrase it to this: *Those who find only their ego-life, will lose their God awareness, but those who put down their ego-life will find divine fullness of life.* And that's what Jesus said he came to bring, life in abundance. But none of this happens overnight, it all takes time. It's about growing the fruits of the spirit – love, joy, peace, patience, kindness, generosity, faithfulness, gentleness, and self-control. It is literally a transformation of the mind, a rewiring of the brain, so that no longer do we react from a defensive, hard-hearted place, but we open ourselves to divine grace and react to life's circumstances with compassion, with the fruit of the spirit. This is the Wisdom path that Jesus blazed for us.

In 1983, Matthew Fox wrote an influential book called *Original Blessing*, in which he tried to give some corrective teaching to counteract the all-pervasive influence of the doctrine of Original Sin. The good news is we are blessed originally! This is the story in the first chapter of Genesis. Genesis begins with six clear statements of original blessing or inherent goodness (Genesis 1:10–31), and the words 'original sin' are not in the New Testament. Repeatedly, we are told after the days of creation 'And God saw that it was good.' How did we miss that? It still is good, but we are making a mess for future generations unless we do something about it. The first story of creation shows the basis of ecology – a world in balance. God's order in the six days or periods of creation balances day and night, light and dark, water and land, work and rest – every part relying on every other part. Day one has echoes in day four, day two in day five, day three in day six. Utterly good and beautiful! But it's all in a delicate balance.

Every seventh day man and their animals were ordered to rest. This was considered so important that it is one of the Ten

Commandments. The Law of Moses taught care of the land –
every seventh year it was to be left fallow. There was no intensive
farming there. Leviticus Chapter 25 even describes a Jubilee
Year. This dealt largely with land, property, and property rights.
According to Leviticus, slaves and prisoners would be freed, and
debts would be forgiven. The need for equality was recognised.
The Bible teaches that we are not to take advantage of the weak,
the poor, the widows and orphans. In particular, the Israelites
were not to harvest their fields to the edge, but were to leave a
border for the poor to glean. This is compassionate generosity.
Moreover, Moses was given strict laws of hygiene, which were
designed to prevent the spread of diseases such as leprosy. It
was very early health care policy.

No, Genesis is not to blame for humanity messing up the globe.
The ancient teaching was to manage the ecosystem's resources
responsibly, to care for animals, fish, birds, plants and the very
ground itself. But profit and pleasure motives led to plunder
and pollution. It is actually in our own self-interest to care for
the world we live in, along with everything in it, but what has
happened? The ozone layer got depleted. Big business is bent
on force-feeding us experimental genetically modified foods.
The once-conquered plagues like tuberculosis are on the rise.
Auto-immune system health problems are rapidly increasing.
Creatures are becoming extinct. Land and sea is polluted with
chemicals and plastic. Rubbish disposal is at crisis point. Famine
is rife in lands that are already in debt to richer nations. We can
trace most of these issues down to human complacency and
greed. There is now a growing awareness that our consumerist
way of life has to change, and change quickly and drastically.
The Extinction Rebellion movement is one sign of this growing
consciousness.

The Church has not been active in this area until recently. It
has simply not addressed the issues in the past. The green lobby
has grown and grown and has looked to other areas of spirituality

to support it, because the Church did not seem to have a voice. The tide is slowly turning, Christianity is now expressing its ecological concern, in more than just a thanksgiving service at Harvest time. But does it match up to the Green's standards? Here's Jonathan Porritt's 'Minimum Criteria for Being Green', which he wrote back in 1984. How are we shaping up?

Green Criteria:

- a reverence for the Earth and all its creatures.
- a willingness to share the world's wealth amongst all its people.
- prosperity to be achieved through sustainable alternatives to the rat race of economic growth.
- lasting security to be achieved through non-nuclear defence strategies and considerably reduced arms spending.
- a rejection of materialism and the destructive values of industrialism.
- a recognition of the rights of future generations in our use of all resources.
- an emphasis on socially useful, personally rewarding work, enhanced by human-scale technology.
- an emphasis on personal growth and spiritual development.
- respect for the gentler side of human nature.
- open, participatory democracy at every level of society.
- recognition of the crucial importance of significant reduction in population levels.
- harmony between people of every race, colour and creed.
- a non-nuclear, low-energy strategy based on conservation, greater efficiency and renewable resources.
- an emphasis on self-reliance and decentralised communities
-

(Jonathan Porritt, 1984. *Seeing Green: The Politics of Ecology*

Explained. Oxford: Blackwell)

Gaia and the Planet Earth

Back in the 1970s, James Lovelock came up with a scientific theory about the planet, to which he gave the name the Gaia Theory. Little did he know how this would take off and be adopted by ecologists and environmentalists to describe the nature of the biosphere as a living entity. Basically, his theory was that the biosphere behaves *as if* it is a living organism. It self-regulates and maintains a delicate balance that helps to maintain and perpetuate the conditions for life on the planet. He named the idea after Gaia, the primordial goddess who personified the Earth in Greek mythology. If he'd called it the Lovelock Theory, it might have sunk without trace!

Naming his theory after Gaia spoke directly into many religious traditions that see the Earth as a living entity, with a god or goddess embodying it. 'Mother Nature' is another expression of this. Within the teachings of the Perennial Wisdom tradition, that is exactly how the planet is seen, as a body of consciousness of a much exalted level.

As related in the previous chapter, scientifically, consciousness is beginning to be seen as the universal informational domain from which all material reality emerges. There is only one consciousness and all matter exists in this divine matrix of consciousness, and hence all matter has some elementary consciousness of its own. For instance, experiments have shown that plants share in consciousness to some degree and will react to other plants being mistreated and to their owner's emotional states. In this mode of thinking, the Earth itself has a vast form of consciousness. Not the same as ours and on a much greater scale, but it is still part of the consciousness of God and has an aliveness and beingness of a much greater nature than our little lives, though we are part of it.

It can be a diversion from the real process of transformation in our realm of existence to get caught up in too much speculation and theorising about other realms. The Wisdom tradition of Christianity, upheld by many of the mystics through the ages, takes this understanding. God's consciousness pervades all, is in all, sustains all in being. It is the Ground of Being, and all manifest reality shines forth from the Divine Source. Cynthia Bourgeault, an Episcopalian priest and Wisdom teacher, encapsulates it in her book *The Wisdom Way of Knowing* (p. 53),

> As we begin orienting ourselves on the Wisdom road map, it is with the recognition that our manifest universe is not simply an 'object' created by a wholly other God out of the effluence of his love, but is that love itself, made manifest in the only possible way it can, in the dimensions of energy and form. The created realm is not an artifact but an instrument through which the divine life becomes perceptible to itself. It's the way the score gets transformed into the music.

So Gaia is not just a scientific theory. If the Earth is conscious, we have to realize that we are not separate from it but are an integral part of this conscious Earth, this body. In relation to the Earth-consciousness, we are tiny, but are having a significant effect in terms of pollution and global warming. It's a bit like the relationship of our cells to our whole body. We are enormous, God-like, compared to our cells, but the behaviour of our cells can significantly affect our whole body, causing illness. The body may then react to reduce or eliminate unwanted or bothersome cells. Is this the future that faces us on the planet? Or can we change our ways to avoid the planet having to reassert its delicate balance by creating some cataclysmic events for humanity?

Oneness

The New Story is that we are all part of the One Consciousness which holds everything in being, permeates everything and is the One Life in which we live and move and have our being – to quote St Paul! We are all one, not just with the rest of humanity, but with the whole of the biosphere, the planet. We are an interconnected whole. As Dr. Jude Currivan says in her book *The Cosmic Hologram* (p. 233), 'Consciousness isn't something we have, it's what we and the whole world are.'

This is what the mystics and religious have been saying for millennia, in their own language and understanding! Their understanding is based on a human experience, something possible for all humanity. Not everyone has had that human experience, but for those who have, it is life-changing. What is it? It is when we are taken up in a feeling and knowing of such awe and wonder that we *know* we are one with everything, and are held in love. It is the mystical experience of being at one with the Divine, unity awareness, oneness. It is a normal human experience, something possible for anyone to have, given the right conditions. But, it is then interpreted in the understanding of the time and culture and context of that person. So the articulation of these experiences takes on the clothing of the religious and moral system of the time. The problem is, we can mistake the clothing for the inner human experience, which leads us to imagine differences where actually none exist. The experience of oneness in Christianity is the same as that in Hinduism, Islam, Buddhism, Taoism, or any other spiritual path.

This oneness is seen as the heartbeat of life and is also recognised within the ecological movement. In the early seventies, the Norwegian philosopher Arne Naess made the distinction between what he called 'shallow' ecology and 'deep' ecology. Shallow ecology sees everything as human-centred and focusses on how useful or not this or that is for us. It stems from the Newtonian world-view and is seen in the religious traditions of the West, where domination and subjugation of the environment has been the prevailing trend. Deep ecology sees humanity as part of the total natural environment and gives intrinsic value to all beings, plant and animal. Everything in nature is fundamentally interconnected and interdependent. The 'self' is no longer seen as an isolated separate individual. We exist in a living biosphere which we share with each other and all other species of life. This view is summed up in Joanna Macy's phrase, 'the greening of the self'.

Here we have the opening of a new understanding of our place in the world. We can no longer behave as if our actions do not have consequences for the rest of the natural world. We are undergoing a major shift in human consciousness, moving up into a higher gear. We have to become responsible citizens in this global city, coexisting with all other Life, because, at the deepest level, we are one with all Life, as it is held in existence by the Divine Plan.

Questions for Reflection

1. Think back to when you first became aware of the impending climate crisis. What was your reaction?
2. Have you or your friends and relatives had any personal health problems that you would put down to pollution or other environmental factors? What were they and what was the cause?
3. What changes would you like to see in Christian teaching with regard to the environment and ecological systems?

Practice
An Awareness Walk...

What is this life if, full of care,
We have no time to stand and stare...
No time to turn at Beauty's glance,
And watch her feet, how they can dance.
William Henry Davies

WALK for exercise first, take some good strong breaths of fresh air. Resist hurry. Slow down to a stroll. Don't try to think, just BE in God's creation.

BE AWARE of the light, the shadow, the warmth of the sun or the cold air, the cloud formations, the colour of the clouds and sky.

LOOK
At patterns, shapes, height, depth, thicknesses.
At colours, shades of green, leaves, grasses, flowers, trees.
At shapes of buildings, roofs, tiles.
For stillness and movement – insects, birds, animals.

TOUCH
Sharp, smooth, grass, stone, bark.
Textures in petals, leaves.
Soil, water, rock.
If you like, remove footwear and let your feet feel.

SMELL
Scent of flowers, herbs, pine needles, earth, leaf mould.
'Nice' smells and not so nice smells.

LISTEN
Shut your eyes, stand still or lie down.
Water, birds, insects, traffic, far-off sounds, near-by sounds, your own breathing.

FOCUS
On one thing more closely, something that particularly draws you.
Become more aware of it, really look at it, take it in, God's creation, held in his compassionate consciousness.

GIVE THANKS

Give thanks to God for his creation, its detail and intricacy and beauty, and for his love and light holding it in being.

You may wish to draw or paint or write; bring something back – a twig or stone – as a focus.

Signposts for Further Study
Books

Thomas Berry, 2009. *The Sacred Universe: Earth, Spirituality, and Religion in the Twenty-first Century*. New York: Columbia University Press

Thomas Berry, 2009. *The Christian Future and the Fate of Earth*. New York: Orbis Books

Ilia Delio, Pamela Wood, Keith Warner, 2008. *Care for Creation: A Franciscan Spirituality of the Earth*. Ann Arbour MI: Servant Books

Matthew Fox, 1983. *Original Blessing: A Primer in Creation Spirituality*. Santa Fe: Bear & Co.

Vaughan-Lee, Llewellyn (ed.), 2016. *Spiritual Ecology – The Cry of the Earth*. Point Reys Station CA: Golden Sufi Center

Websites

Green Christian (name changed from Christian Ecology Link). They have a very helpful set of resources and information on climate change. https://greenchristian.org.uk/

Green Spirit emerged from a strand of Christian mysticism influenced by Matthew Fox's Creation-Centred Spirituality. It now has a broad appeal to those both within and beyond the Christian tradition. https://www.greenspirit.org.uk/

Center for the Story of the Universe, founded by Brian Swimme, inspired by the work of Thomas Berry: 'We are between stories. The Old Story – the account of how the world came to be and how we fit into it – is not functioning properly, and we have not (yet) learned the New Story.' The new creation story is rooted in the new science in general, and cosmology. http://www.storyoftheuniverse.org

The Work That Reconnects. Drawing from deep ecology, systems theory and spiritual traditions, the Work That Reconnects builds motivation, creativity, courage and solidarity for the transition to a sustainable human culture. First emerging in 1978, this pioneering, open-source body of work has its roots in the teachings and experiential methods of Joanna Macy. http://workthatreconnects.org/

Chapter 5

Christianity Expanding

Here is a little story I found on the Internet many years ago.

One spring day, there was a blind man sitting on the steps of a building with a sign by his feet that read:

'I am blind, please help'.

A graphic designer was walking by him and noticed the man only had a few coins in his hat. He dropped a few more coins in and, without asking for his permission, picked up the sign, turned it around and wrote another message. He placed the sign by his feet and left.

That afternoon, the graphic designer returned by the blind man and noticed that his hat was full of notes and coins. The blind man recognised his footsteps and asked if it was he who had re-written his sign and he wanted to know what he wrote on it. The designer responded, 'Nothing that wasn't true, I just reworded it.' He smiled and went on his way. The blind man never knew but his new sign read:

TODAY IS SPRING AND I CANNOT SEE IT

Expressing the same message in different ways can revolutionise things. What is the message that Christianity is trying to convey? My view of it is something like this:

- There is a God of love in whom we live and move and have our being.
- Jesus showed us what it is like to fulfil human potential, to be a god-filled human being, which led to his death and changed the information pattern, the morphic field, for all humanity. He demonstrated for us the Christ path.
- In this one man, humanity and the Christ aspect of God were joined. Divine Love and Wisdom shone forth in

human form.

- In following the path blazed by Jesus the Christ, we are all on a journey of transformation into wholeness.
- There are new spiritual energies coming in at this auspicious time which are raising the consciousness of humanity.
- This is the way forward for the human race, to be slowly transformed for the betterment of humanity.
- The gospel message should be, 'Awaken now to the reality of the divine presence within and embrace the mind of Christ.'

The message we are trying to convey is crucial. It may mean that we need to revisit some of our basic theology of God the Father and God the Son. For instance, as previously mentioned, many serious theologians now question the idea of Christ dying on the cross as a *punishment* for our sin, the retribution of an angry God, because that is not the God revealed by Christ, nor is it a very acceptable way of looking at it in today's world. There are many others ways of thinking about Christ's death on the cross, all stemming from different ways of interpreting the Bible. The theory (and it is only a theory) of Jesus being a substitution and taking the punishment that is due to us all was not fully articulated until 1098 by St Anselm in his search to provide a rational argument for the necessity of the incarnation and death of Jesus.

Anselm used a cultural model drawn from his time and place: the relationship of a medieval lord to his peasants. If a peasant disobeyed the lord, could the lord simply forgive if he wanted to? No, because that might imply that disobedience didn't matter that much. Instead, compensation must be made. Anselm used this model for our relationship with God. We sin and therefore deserve to be punished, but God also loves us and wants to forgive us. This theory says the price of sin must be paid, so Jesus the sinless one steps in as a substitution. That's the feudal logic. The good news is that we do not have to stay with this medieval, feudal model! We can change the way we see it. The Eastern Orthodox Church never accepted the idea that Christ died to give God 'satisfaction' as taught by Anselm, or as a punitive substitute as taught by the Reformers. In their view, sin is separation from God, who is the source of all life, and is its own punishment, capable of imprisoning the soul in an existence without quality and fullness of life, without anything good, and without hope. Life on Earth is a privilege given for our souls to grow and learn, and gives humankind opportunity to make a real choice: separation or union. Ultimately, union will happen – which brings in the concept of rebirth, more of which later.

Actually, although animals were sacrificed in the Judaic temple, it can be argued that the purpose of this was not about payment for sin, but it was an act of making something sacred by giving it as a gift to God. Sacrifices were not about something being killed as an appeasement to a wrathful God, but were offerings made to give thanks, to purify and to reconcile their own inner feelings of guilt. Seen metaphorically, these acts are not about a transaction, they are expressions of transformation.

I vividly remember one of our daughters who, as a six-year-old, could not bring herself to say sorry when she did something wrong. We gave her every opportunity to express some form of repentance, but she couldn't bring herself to say anything, even though she was totally forgiven and loved to bits by us. One day, she took herself off and came back with a picture of Lady and the Tramp that she had carefully traced from the video cover picture, and the word 'Sorry' scrawled large underneath. She offered this up to us without a word, just a little smile! This was a moment of transformation for her, not a transaction for us. What she offered up was a symbol of a deep change in her.

The transformation that Jesus undertook in his life and death was on behalf of all humanity, forging a new path, affecting all of us. The sacrifice Jesus made was of his lower desire-nature in order to live from his divine soul-self. It was not a transaction in payment to satisfy the requirements of, in the best version, the sense of justice in a loving God, or, in the worst version, the appeasement of an angry dictator God. It was a life-affirming, path-blazing, all-loving act of sacrificial giving.

Transforming the Mind

Human nature is a complex thing, but it is often talked of in two ways: the lower self and the higher self, or the selfish, self-centred nature and the selfless, higher nature, or the ego-mind and the Christ-mind. St Paul talks very often of the flesh and the Spirit, making the same distinction:

> For those who live according to the flesh set their minds on the things of the flesh, but those who live according to the Spirit set their minds on the things of the Spirit. To set the mind on the flesh is death, but to set the mind on the Spirit is life and peace. (Romans 8:5–6)

To set the mind on the flesh is death? This is not physical death, so what is Paul talking about? I think he is meaning death to the presence of God, the awareness of the divine, death to the awareness of the One Life that permeates the whole universe and holds us all in being. The Christian journey is to move from this death to recognising the presence of God, from living purely 'in the flesh' to an aliveness, and an awakening to the deep love of God that exists at the heart of everything. Paul recognises that not everyone is there, and there are many different stages on the path:

> And so, brothers and sisters, I could not speak to you as spiritual people, but rather as people of the flesh, as infants in Christ. I fed you with milk, not solid food, for you were

not ready for solid food. Even now you are still not ready, for you are still of the flesh. For as long as there is jealousy and quarrelling among you, are you not of the flesh, and behaving according to human inclinations? (1 Corinthians 3:1–3)

Are we ready for solid food, or do we still get lost in quarrels, living in the lower self, responding to the ego, letting pride or arrogance get in the way? Me first, selfishness, greed, anger, violence. Can we still identify those elements of lower, self-centred ego-mind in us? How do we match up to Paul's instructions to the Colossian Church?

You have clothed yourselves with the new self, which is being renewed in knowledge according to the image of its creator... Clothe yourselves with compassion, kindness, humility, meekness, and patience. Bear with one another and, if anyone has a complaint against another, forgive each other; just as the Lord has forgiven you, so you also must forgive. Above all, clothe yourselves with love, which binds everything together in perfect harmony. (Colossians 3:10–15)

Once we put on the new self, we have a common bond, we are all one *en Christos*, to use Paul's phrase. We begin to put on those clothes that Paul speaks of – compassion, kindness, humility, meekness (meaning gentleness), and patience. We are changed, transformed.

Do not be conformed to this world, but be transformed by the renewing of your minds, so that you may discern what is the will of God—what is good and acceptable and perfect. (Romans 12:2)

Paul says it in lots of different ways. Be transformed by the renewing of your mind, put on the new clothes, clothe yourself with love, leave the life of the flesh and enter the life of the Spirit. They are all saying the same thing – that following the Jesus path means to awaken to a new way of being that leaves behind the old ego-nature, the selfish self, to enter into the Christ-self.

> For who has known the mind of the Lord so as to instruct him? But we have the mind of Christ. (1 Corinthians 2:16)

The mind of Christ is the Spirit mind, the higher nature, a different level of consciousness. If we can centre ourselves in that level of compassionate loving consciousness, then our whole lives begin to operate in a different way. We begin to see people in a different light; we react differently to what others say. It is a radical way that Jesus taught: a radical love of God and neighbour, operating from a different level of consciousness. Jesus called this way of life, symbolically, the kingdom of God. He invited his listeners to enter into this kingdom of God in the here and now. That is what the Christian life is really about: transformation, being changed. Repentance actually means changing the way we think, developing the contemplative mind, moving beyond our small minds and entering into the Divine Life.

Living in the Contemplative Mind

The result of moving the centre of consciousness from the surface lower self to the deeper, higher self is that we live from a place of contemplative reflection. The ability to stand back and calmly observe our inner and outer dramas, without rushing to judgement or solution, is sometimes called being the 'inner observer' or the 'witnessing presence'. It is a form of dying to the self, or self-emptying. This type of calm, egoless seeing is invariably characteristic of people at the highest levels of doing and loving in all cultures and religions and is a hallmark of spiritual maturity. They are the ones we call sages or wise women or holy men. Many of us call it the contemplative mind;

Paul calls it 'the mind of Christ'. It is an alternative, deeper consciousness to our ordinary, calculating mind which judges who is okay and who is not okay. This ego-mind sees everything in dualities, opposites and categories. We use it all the time in our daily living – but we do not have to dwell in it. One of the methods to retrain our way of thinking so that it is not caught up in the endless round of surface thoughts is meditation. Often, meditation and contemplation are used interchangeably. Meditation is the technique; contemplation is the resultant form of prayer. There are many techniques of meditation including breath work, repeating a sacred word, chanting, using a seed thought and many others. The technique is working if it results in a state of contemplation, bringing the focus of the mind to that higher/deeper place from which compassion flows and where unitive consciousness abides.

Living in the contemplative mind is living from a soul perspective. The soul is that divine expression of who we are that inhabits our personality. Our personality is made up of our mind, our emotions and our physical body. When we die, the personality dies or fades away, but the soul-consciousness goes on. If we can access the finer vibrations of the contemplative mind, we are reaching into the soul and touching into the eternal presence of the Divine, the spark of Spirit within us, which can then lead and guide us in our daily living. This is the purpose of meditation, a universal practice which has undergone a huge rediscovery in the last fifty years within the Christian tradition. It can be a daily practice for our spiritual development.

Love-Wisdom Teacher

Jesus was, above all, a teacher of Love-Wisdom. I put these two terms together, because his central teaching was about love, but his style was that of a wisdom teacher. He spoke in parables and pithy sayings mostly, which made people think for themselves, work it out for themselves and own it for themselves. If you want a meat pie to feed some friends, you can either cook it yourself or buy one. If you decide to cook your own pie, you might do some recipe research, decide what would go best in it, then you chop all the vegetables and meat and make the pastry. You labour over a hot stove for a while and then you wait to get the delicious thing out of the oven. You will be much more committed to the meal and care more about its flavour and appearance than if you just buy a pre-packed, frozen pie and whack it in the oven! Similarly, if you've thought deeply about an issue of faith, read a bit about it, chewed it over, looked at it in different ways until you come to make your own mind up, you will have a much stronger faith than if you just accept the pre-packed version that the vicar or pastor serves up. Thinking through what you believe brings our faith alive, fans it into flame. Parables make you think and work at it yourself. It was how wisdom teachers taught.

They also taught by using pithy sayings. Jesus is quoted in John's gospel as saying: 'I came that they may have life, and have it abundantly' (John 10:10). God wants the best for us, wants to see us whole, healed, and living life in all its fullness. Salvation is about that growth into wholeness, about the transformation to a better way of being, in which we become less self-centred and more self-less. I come back again to Jesus' enigmatic saying 'Those who find their life will lose it, and those who lose their life for my sake will find it' (Matthew 10:39). This is recorded in all four gospels. It is about this letting go of the egoic, self-centred life and moving, transforming, to a better way of selfless love and compassion. We begin to operate from a different centre within us, we are brought to a better place, we are 'saved'.

That is the potential for each and every one of us – to have abundant life in all its fullness. For all sorts of reasons, it doesn't always work out that way, but the potential is still there. Sometimes that potential is not reached until after the grave, but ultimately we will all know fullness of life. It should be the aspiration of every Christian to allow God, working in us, to change us to be more Christ-like, a more whole person, living in fullness.

Salvation and Betterment

If we can invent the average churchgoer for a moment (if there is such a being) and ask them what salvation means, I guess many would say that you are saved by believing in Jesus and thus will have a place in heaven when you die. But looking a bit closer, salvation is not so much about the life to come as the life here and now. The word salvation comes from a Latin word meaning wholeness or healing – the same root as we get the word 'salve', a healing ointment (also salute, salubrious, Shalom, Salaam). In its broadest sense, salvation is about being made whole and healed, being brought to a better place. Healed in our relationship with God, healed in our relationships with each other and, in an inner sense, with ourselves, an inner healing. It is this transformation to a level of loving compassionate consciousness that the message of Jesus is about. If we look at the Bible, we find the message of transformation expressed in all sorts of different ways. It is about:

- Moving from darkness to light
- Receiving true sight
- Being born again
- Liberation for captives
- Freedom from bondage
- Healing from our infirmities
- Hearts of stone being replaced with hearts of flesh
- Moving from death to life
- Moving from emptiness to fullness
- Being made in the image of Christ, putting on the mind of Christ

In many ways, the original idea of salvation was simply to be brought to a better place now. The salvation of the Israelites was to be brought from slavery in Egypt to the promised land of milk and honey in Canaan. Our salvation is to be brought to a better place on our journey through life, which Jesus called the kingdom of God. He also said it is around us and within us, if only we can awaken to it. So we are to be transformed, saved, rescued, by the renewing of our minds when we give ourselves totally over to God, when we move into a different level of consciousness, from flesh to Spirit, from self-centred to God-centred, from ego to soul. It sounds a bit of a tall order, doesn't it – but actually, the way to do it is well-known – it is all about walking the Christian path, walking the talk!

That is the reason for traditional Christian practices of prayer, Bible reading, worship and, I would like to add, *contemplative prayer or meditation*. It is to spend time in the presence and awareness of God, in humility and the surrender and letting go of ego. What this does is build the framework that allows the Divine presence and energies to work in our lives. If you want to learn to play a musical instrument, you can listen to it being played, you can own one yourself, you can buy all the teach-yourself books, you can talk to musicians, but none of that will make much difference. You won't learn to play it until you get to grips with the instrument itself, giving attention to it regularly, gradually building a relationship with the instrument until you know it intimately, until you love your instrument.

So too with God and putting on the mind of Christ. Following the Christian way is about building the form which allows our inner selves to move the level of consciousness from flesh to spirit – expressing love for God by paying attention to God. All the things that Christians do are ways of paying attention to God:

- Bible study and devotional reading
- Prayer, reflection, contemplation

- Worshipping together
- Acts of compassion and justice in the world

Christian practice is about walking with God-awareness, aligning ourselves with that compassionate consciousness, and then acting with compassion to bring about peace and justice in this troubled world. It's not just about believing in God and being a 'good person' – it is about how one *becomes* a good person through the practice of love and goodwill. The destiny of each one of us is to become a compassionate, transformed, renewed person, for the betterment of all.

Sacrifice and Substitution

I want to delve into this subject a little deeper. Judaism in the time of Jesus was steeped in the idea of animal sacrifice to atone for the people's sin. But slowly, a new understanding developed for the followers of Jesus – a change from the old way of high priests and sacrifice, to the new way of Christ.

The old way was pretty gruesome – every day, the priests had to make animal sacrifices for the people – day in, day out, twice a day, morning and evening. It was set out in Numbers 28:3–8. Every morning and evening, a male lamb, without spot or blemish, was offered as a burnt offering, along with offerings of flour and oil, wine and incense. It went on relentlessly, day after day. In addition, there were extra offerings on the Sabbath, and monthly offerings, and when it came to the feasts, there was a veritable bloodbath of bulls, lambs, pigeons and all. It became a kind of priestly tread-mill of sacrifice, and all this because it was thought to atone for the sins of the people. There was no end to the process.

Yet many of the biblical prophets said that God did not want their sacrifices. He wanted a change in behaviour, for his people to behave with compassion, to show mercy and care for the oppressed. That was much more important than any sacrifice.

'The multitude of your sacrifices—what are they to me?' says the LORD. 'I have more than enough of burnt offerings, of rams and the fat of fattened animals; I have no pleasure in the blood of bulls and lambs and goats. Stop bringing meaningless offerings! Your incense is detestable to me. New Moons, Sabbaths and convocations—I cannot bear your worthless assemblies. Wash and make yourselves clean. Take your evil deeds out of my sight; stop doing wrong. Learn to do right; seek justice. Defend the oppressed. Take up the cause of the fatherless; plead the case of the widow.' (Isaiah 1:11,13,16,17)

For I desire mercy, not sacrifice, and acknowledgment of God rather than burnt offerings. (Hosea 6:6)

With what shall I come before the LORD and bow down before the exalted God? Shall I come before him with burnt offerings, with calves a year old? Will the LORD be pleased with thousands of rams, with ten thousand rivers of olive oil? Shall I offer my firstborn for my transgression, the fruit of my body for the sin of my soul? He has shown you, O mortal, what is good. And what does the LORD require of you? To act justly and to love mercy and to walk humbly with your God. (Micah 6:6–8)

This was also the emphasis of the teaching of Jesus, to change our behaviour and to act with compassion. The collection of his sayings known as the Sermon on the Mount is the most famous teaching passage in Matthew Chapters Five to Seven, and its message is to go beyond the message of the Hebrew scriptures and in doing so to bring them to fulfilment. In those three chapters, we are all encouraged to:

- Let our light shine forth. (Matthew 5:16)

- Control anger and behave responsibly in our relationships, seeking reconciliation. (Mathew 5:21–26)
- Be responsible in our sexual relationships. (Matthew 5 27–32)
- Be honest and trustworthy. (Matthew 5:33–37)
- Not to seek retaliation or revenge, but to understand the motivation of the other. (Matthew 5:38–42)
- Love the unlovable. (Matthew 5:43–48)
- Be generous. (Matthew 6:1–4)
- Be prayerful and spiritually oriented in our lives. (Matthew 6:5–24, 7:7–11))
- Trust that God is working in and amongst us. (Matthew 6:25–34)
- Eliminate our judgemental attitudes. (Matthew 7:1–6)
- To obey the Golden Rule, present in all major faiths, 'Do to others as you would have them do to you.' (Matthew 7:12)

This teaching is all about how to live in harmonious human relationships – how to get on with each other! The only sacrifice that is required here is the sacrifice of pride, vanity, greed, envy, hate, revenge and all the other negative aspects of the human psyche. Jesus was teaching a higher way, the narrow way that he mentions in Matthew 7:14. It is a movement of a person's consciousness, a deliberate act of self-sacrifice to follow this way. How satisfying it is to seek revenge! How powerful we can feel when we give out a good put-down to someone we dislike! These are the attitudes and feelings we each have to sacrifice and move beyond to find the narrow way of compassion.

The temple altar sacrifices of the past were to be replaced by a more enlightened self-sacrifice, letting go of those aspects of the lower human nature in order to become a better human being, a better human race. It is a sacrifice of the lower human nature on the altar of the heart. How have we done with that? Not so good. Yet if we look back at human behaviour of the past, we begin to see we are progressing – human consciousness is changing to a more compassionate stance. We only have to look back 500 years to see what we would now class as inhumane treatment of all sorts, brutality, torture, executions and tribal thinking at all levels. We have changed. We still have a long way to go, but gradually human consciousness is progressing.

The Sacrifice of Jesus

What about the sacrifice of Jesus? He undoubtedly had sacrificed his lower human nature. You might ask, did he have one? Wasn't he sinless? Traditional Christian teaching tells us that he was fully human, not just a bit human. The teaching also tells us that this fully human person was also fully divine. He was living out the full human potential for divinity, demonstrating the highest possible human path and blazing the way for all humanity to follow. He was a way-shower, a trail-blazer. But his death on the cross was understandably interpreted in the light of the Temple sacrifices. In the Old Testament sacrifices, unblemished, perfect lambs were sacrificed repeatedly by the temple priests. The New Testament writers make the link by seeing the death of Christ as the unblemished, sinless, perfect Lamb of God making the one perfect and sufficient sacrifice for the sins of the world. In the letter to the Hebrews, he is seen as both the sacrifice and the high priest making the sacrifice. I believe Jesus came to make a sacrifice that did not need repeating, but *following*. Not that we all should die on the cross! The primary sacrifice Jesus made was his life, by living in a way that showed the love of God, and living out a way of self-sacrifice and total surrender. As a fully human being, he must have had an egoic nature which he was tempted to assert at times; otherwise he would not be human. But he chose the narrow way; he sacrificed his self-centred desire nature. It led to his death as he was uncompromising on this path in his devotion to God. In his death, he achieved a major breakthrough for both himself and for all humanity.

(I have written in much more detail about this and the theory of morphic resonance in my previous book *Blue Sky God: The Evolution of Science and Christianity*.)

We are all called to live that life of sacrifice of the lower human nature, opening the way for lives and relationships of compassion and loving understanding, forgiveness and goodwill towards all. It is a way of transformation that can change the world.

Eternal Matters

Heaven and hell are still quoted in traditional Christianity as the eternal destinations for humanity. But how did this stark dualistic division arise? Does this fit with the understanding that God loves his creation. Would God consign some to eternal torture? What is hell? Specifically, what is 'the hell of fire' that Jesus often spoke of (Matthew 5:22, 18:9 NRSV)? The word *Gehenna,* rendered here as *hell of fire,* is the Greek version of the Hebrew *Ge-Hinnom,* or Valley of Hinnom. This was a deep, narrow glen to the south of Jerusalem. It was there that the idolatrous Israelites sacrificed their children to Molech (2 Kings 23:10). Later, it became the common rubbish dump of the city, into which the bodies of criminals, carcasses of animals, and all sorts of filth were cast. It smouldered ceaselessly. Because of its depth and narrowness, and the fire and smoke, it became a symbol of the future punishment of the wicked.

As fire was the characteristic of the place, it was called *the Gehenna of fire.* It should be carefully distinguished from Hades, which is never used for the place of punishment, but for the *place of departed spirits,* without reference to their moral condition. That was the Greek word used for Sheol, the place of the dead in the Hebrew Scriptures – a shadowy silent pit to which all the dead go, both the righteous and the unrighteous, regardless of the moral choices made in life, a place of stillness and darkness cut off from life and from the Hebrew God.

In early Christianity, this distinction was lost. Hell and the ultimate fate of those consigned to it was described in different ways. Some theologians, such as Origen and Eusebius, taught that eventually all evil human beings and even Satan himself would be restored to unity with God or universal salvation. Other teachers believed that hell was a temporary state of being where some souls would be purified and others annihilated. Unfortunately, the image that prevailed was that hell was where the souls of the damned suffered torturous and unending punishment. This was reinforced in the middle ages by Dante's gruesome imagery in his 'Divine Comedy'.

However, coming more up to date, in 1995 the Church of England Doctrine Commission wrote in their report 'The Mystery of Salvation' that hell is more likely a place of total non-being outside of God and that heaven is open to people of other faiths. The rationale is that if a person totally denies the existence of the Divine, the God in whom we live and move and have our being, then stepping outside that sustaining force means we cease to exist. If a person believes in some further divine power, then they are held in being. Some progress then! Although stated as the official position of the Doctrine Commission, it seems to have had little impact on Church-going Christian belief.

Heaven is seen in many ways, but there is no definitive version, other than it being a place we go after death to be in God's presence. But the kingdom of heaven, or realm of God, is spoken of as being here, now, amongst and within us. Jesus spoke about the kingdom of heaven or of God more than anything else. It was central to his teaching, linked with repentance. The first words of Jesus in Mark's gospel are 'The kingdom of God is near. Repent and believe the good news' (Mk 1:15). The act of penitence is at the heart of the Anglican and Roman liturgies, confession followed by absolution. However, the meaning of the word contains a surprise. The Greek word is *metanoia*. But it doesn't mean feeling sorrowful for doing or thinking bad things.

It doesn't just mean 'to turn around'. It isn't just about starting out again with God. The word can be broken down into two parts, *meta* and *noia*. *Meta* can mean either 'beyond' or 'large', and noia is 'mind', so it is really saying 'go beyond the mind' or 'go into the large mind'. The repentance that Jesus is talking about is to go beyond ourselves, to enter into the mind, the consciousness, of God, to come to a new level of awareness, or, as St Paul put it 'to be transformed by the renewing of your mind' (Romans 12:2). It is a deep inner change in the way we act and think.

In today's terms, Paul was really talking about us ascending to a new vibratory level of awareness, going beyond our ego-centred mind, getting out of our self-centredness and entering a new way of being, entering the large mind, the consciousness of God. This is transformation. The kingdom of God was Jesus' shorthand for the whole message. The kingdom of God is near, is within you. When you repent, when you come close to God, when you enter the consciousness of God, when you love your neighbour, when you feel compassion for the world, when you can forgive those who hurt you, then you are entering God's kingdom, you are being changed, transformed, refined, you are moving up onto God's resonant frequency, you are beginning to fulfil the God-given potential that you have as a human being, you are aligning yourself with Christ, you are becoming God's child, you recognise Christ within you. However we want to express it. We can get lost in doctrinal arguments about these things but the main message of Jesus was not to talk about it, but to live it out. Not to be moral upstanding people living a 'good' life, but to be compassionate people, full of life and light, giving energy and life to others.

Universal Salvation and Rebirth

Since the 1960s and the influx to the West of Eastern faith traditions, the notion of universal salvation has come much more to the fore again. This puts ultimate destinations such as heaven and hell into an entirely different eternal understanding. Going beyond traditional Christian teaching for a moment, this is often coupled with the idea of reincarnation or rebirth. In this model, there is no hell other than what we put ourselves through. We are given many, many chances to progress through thousands of incarnations, and our progress is slow, but will eventually lead to being at-one with God, Divine union. Being fully aware of the reality of our soul and its divine nature is the ultimate aim for our time in bodily form, as we saw in Jesus. In between incarnations, at a soul level, we learn the lessons from the last incarnation, a kind of life appraisal, which could be seen in a different terminology as God's judgement. We reap what we have sown, so the next life will be determined by past lives, and the Divine Plan is ultimately to bring everything into balance and perfection. All will ultimately be restored to oneness in God. To my mind, this is a much more hopeful and positive way of viewing this reality than thinking some of us will go on to paradise and others to eternal damnation.

Can it be a Christian viewpoint? Christianity has had a chequered history with its views on reincarnation, but it is not ruled out in the Bible. Just because the Bible is not conclusive about various issues does not mean that they are wrong. The Bible is not conclusive about what heaven is, about the Trinity, about slavery, women priests, homosexuality, and a myriad other issues. We have to weigh things up and decide for ourselves – this takes wisdom and discernment.

Reincarnation has not always been so unacceptable to Church doctrine. In the early Church, as doctrinal matters were being formulated, there was a vigorous debate about the pre-existence of souls and transmigration of souls (reincarnation). Some of the early Church Fathers considered reincarnationist thinking and did believe in the pre-existence of souls. People such as Clement of Alexandria (circa 150–215 CE), Justin Martyr (circa 100–165 CE), St Gregory of Nyssa (circa 330–395 CE), Arnobius

(d. circa 330 CE), and St Jerome (circa 342–420 CE) all dabbled with the idea of reincarnation. It was a common Greek belief at the time and was discussed as a Christian possibility, especially by those with some knowledge of Greek philosophy, but it was not adopted officially. Even St Augustine of Hippo, in his *Confessions*, entertained the possibility of reincarnation:

> Did my infancy succeed another age of mine that dies before it? Was it that which I spent within my mother's womb? ...And what before that life again, O God of my joy, was I anywhere or in any body?

The most outspoken and influential early Christian theologian in this area was Origen (circa 185–254 CE). He was one of the most prolific Church Fathers. St Jerome said of him that he was the greatest teacher of the Church after the apostles, and St Gregory of Nyssa honoured him as 'The prince of Christian learning in the third century.' Origen conjectured about transmigration on numerous occasions, but then seemed to step back to a more orthodox stance. Jerome, a leading Church Father in the early fifth century, argued that Origen held to reincarnation.

However, politically, reincarnation had a raw deal back in the sixth century CE, which has affected Christian understanding of it since. Origen had his supporters and 'Origenism' became hotly debated after his death. But it was condemned first at a Council in Alexandria in 400 CE, then later at the Second Council of Constantinople in 553 CE (also known as the 5th Ecumenical Council): 'If anyone asserts the fabulous pre-existence of souls and the monstrous restoration which follows from it, let him be anathema.' The 'monstrous restoration' was the idea of rebirth of the soul.

But was it ever officially ratified? It is thought that there were some political manoeuvrings going on here. This was one of many condemnatory 'anathemas' that were largely politically inspired by Emperor Justinian. In order to make 'good citizens', it was thought best that the people believe they had only one life, then heaven or hell. This would focus them more productively in life and help the empire in its purpose of gaining secular power. Pope Vigilius actually refused to attend on the final day, when the anathemas were given out by the emperor – the pope seemed to be mixed about Origen's views. Some would say the anathemas were *never officially recognised* by the Pope and therefore the Christian Church. Through the last 2000 years, there have been those Christians who have argued in favour of reincarnation, written books about it, and pleaded for the Church to listen again to the arguments. My view is that to believe in reincarnation is not anti-Christian – it adds greatly to Christianity, strengthening it in many ways. Perhaps, in the context and global culture of the twenty-first century, the Church may be prepared to begin its exploration of Christian reincarnation. I hope to write more on this topic in a future book.

New Humanity

In summary, my view is that Christianity needs to expand into a larger framework, that of the Perennial Wisdom philosophy, of which Jesus appeared to be a teacher within the Hebrew tradition. Jesus demonstrated to us a new way for humanity, moving beyond the surface of life with all its egotistical posing and divisions and cravings, to a deeper level of divine transformation. He showed how human beings can rise above their lower nature and approach the whole of life from an inner place of love and compassion, understanding and insight. He was demonstrating a new humanity, where there are no more divisions, where hostility is put to death, where peace is preached to those who are far off and those who are near. It's his basic teaching to love your neighbour, yourself and even your enemy. It is goodwill to all in action. This can only happen in a conscious relationship with the divine, which is why he spent so many long nights in prayer up on the hillsides. Jesus was a fully transformed human being, so much so that he was at one with the divine. His was a call to the oneness of living from an inner place of unity. If we can begin to live life from this place, then we begin to change the world. This is the Christ impetus that is upon us at this time. Humanity has to move into a level of consciousness of goodwill and loving understanding to all if we are to progress on this planet.

Questions for Reflection

1. What signs are there of this new story emerging in the Church?
2. How has your understanding of the life and death of Jesus changed over the years?
3. What are your views on heaven and hell?
4. If you were to write a creed, what would you want to emphasise. Maybe have a go!

Practice
The Great Invocation

This invocation is essentially a prayer, synthesizing the highest desire, aspiration, and spiritual demand of the very soul of humanity. 'No one can use this Invocation or prayer for illumination and for love without causing powerful changes in his own attitudes; his life intention, character and goals will be changed and his life will be altered and made spiritually useful' (Alice A. Bailey, Discipleship in the New Age, Vol. II, p. 168).

From the point of Light within the Mind of God
Let light stream forth into human minds.
Let Light descend on Earth.
From the point of Love within the Heart of God
Let love stream forth into human hearts.
May the Coming One return to Earth.

From the centre where the Will of God is known
Let purpose guide all little human wills —
The purpose which the Great Ones know and serve.
From the centre which we call the human race
Let the Plan of Love and Light work out
And may it seal the door where evil dwells.
Let Light and Love and Power restore the Plan on Earth.

Signposts for Further Study
Books

Bourgeault, C., 2003. *The Wisdom Way of Knowing – Reclaiming and Ancient Tradition to Awaken the Heart.* San Francisco (CA): Jossey-Bass

Bourgeault, C., 2008. *The Wisdom Jesus: Transforming Heart and Mind – a New Perspective on Christ and His Message.* Boston: Shambhala Publications Inc.

Borg, M., 2003. *The Heart of Christianity.* New York: HarperCollins

MacGregor, Don, 2012. *Blue Sky God: The Evolution of Science and Christianity.* Winchester UK: Circle Books

McLaren, Brian, 2010. *A New Kind of Christianity.* New York: Harper-Collins

Marion, Jim, 2000. *Putting on the Mind of Christ: The Inner Work of Christian Spirituality.* Charlottesville VA: Hampton-Roads

Smith, Adrian B., 2005. *Tomorrow's Faith: A New Framework of Christian Belief.* Winchester UK: O Books

Smith, Adrian B., 2005. *Tomorrow's Christian: A New Framework for Christian Living.* Winchester UK: O Books

Teasdale, Wayne, 1999. *The Mystic Heart: Discovering a Universal Spirituality in the World's Religions.* Novato CA: New World Library

Websites

Fr. Richard Rohr, Franciscan priest, a prolific author, heads up the Centre for Action and Contemplation at https://cac.org/

His latest book is *The Universal Christ.*

Revd Dr. Cynthia Bourgeault, Episcopalian priest and author, is known for her Wisdom School Retreats as well as her books. She heads up the Contemplative Society at www.contemplative. org and has her own website at www.cynthiabourgeault.org

Brian McLaren is another author known for his emerging Christianity viewpoint. https://brianmclaren.net

.

Chapter 6

Who or What Is God?

Maybe we should have started with this! It is such a difficult, contentious, yet simple question. Every religion and spirituality has its perspective, yet most of them coincide at the deepest level, which is that whatever name we give to God, it represents the ultimate reality of Being. Within Christianity, we have the concept of the Godhead, the Ground of Being, neither male or female but containing both, and from which everything has been created and formed. St Paul described God to the men of Athens as the one 'in whom we live and move and have our being' (Acts 17.28). This ultimate Being is shown to us in Christian theology in three forms, the Holy Trinity of Father, Son and Holy Spirit. The One becomes the Three. There are many other ways of expressing this. We tend to see everything from our human perspective and personalise the Trinity, but the concept goes well beyond this, which we shall come to later.

Development of the Trinity

The early theologian responsible for the development of the Trinitarian terminology is Tertullian. He invented many new Latin words in his writing, one of which was *Trinitas*, the Trinity, formed of three *personae,* which has invariably been translated into English as 'person'. In the Latin, it literally means 'sounding through' (*per sona*) and was a term used for the masks that were worn by actors in a Roman drama. Each actor could wear different masks so that the audience knew which character they were playing, as one actor may have played more than one character. They *sounded through* the mask. So the term *persona* came to mean 'the role that someone is playing'.

Tertullian was trying to convey the idea that the Godhead is expressed through different roles, or is seen in different ways. The parent God is the one who holds us. God the Son is what a human being filled with God looks like, and God as Spirit is the presence or energy of God in the world. Different roles of the one God.

Later refinements came to the conclusion that Father, Son and Holy Spirit are all of the *substance or essence* of God. But God as Father, Son and Holy Spirit is really a metaphor to help us in our understanding of God. Unfortunately, metaphors are often taken as literal truth. We do not take other metaphors as literal. For instance, 'The Lord is my rock' is a common metaphor in the Bible. It says that God is solid, unmoveable, a solid base for life. It does **not** say that God is grey, hard and rough, maybe with white streaks or sparkly bits, and can often be found sticking out of the ground. We know which parts are true, what qualities of rock are being referred to. God as the Holy Trinity is also a metaphor that has been very helpful as Christianity has evolved and grown in its theology. We should know which bits of the metaphor are true, but the church has had a tendency to become more and more literal in its interpretation of this metaphor, to the extent that it has become a stumbling stone for many, with God literally seen as a father, existing in that human form in a place called heaven, even sitting on a white cloud with his flowing beard. The Holy Spirit becomes a dove, or a ghost, floating about ethereally. Jesus sits there at the Father's right hand. Metaphors easily become concretised, and in doing so, they lose meaning. To quote Revd Dr Cynthia Bourgeault, 'The Trinity is not two men and a bird'!

The Nicene Creed

About a century after Tertullian, in 325 CE, the Council of Nicaea set out to officially define the relationship of the Son to the Father, in response to the teachings of Arius, who said that the Son was subordinate to the Father, not equal. This caused a right old stir, and the Council of Nicaea was called with all the bishops. Led by Bishop Athanasius, the council established the doctrine of the Trinity as orthodoxy – and then condemned everything else as heresy. Before that, there were various versions of Christianity, none of which were seen as being the 'correct' version – people just favoured one or other. It was with the adoption of Christianity as the official religion of the Roman Empire at this time that it began to be closely defined and tied up in doctrine. The creed adopted by the Nicene council described Christ as *'God of God, Light of Light, very God of very God, begotten, not made, being of one substance with the Father.'* And that has been with us since, as the Christian definition of Jesus the Christ.

But how are we to understand it in this day and age? We now know the size of the universe, and the complexity of the sub-atomic particles and forces. We know that mass is energy, $E=mc^2$. Scientists tell us that we are comprised of interacting, communicating vibrational energies that make up our very being. We are vibrational beings of energy.

One way that modern theologians think about it is to see God as 'Being'. Remember the words that God spoke to Moses from the burning bush. Moses asked, 'Who shall I say sent me?'

God said to Moses, 'I AM WHO I AM. Thus you shall say to the Israelites, "I AM has sent me to you."' (Exodus 3:14)

I AM means God is the ultimate 'Being'. God is Life itself. So another way some theologians have of expressing the Trinity is that the Father is understood to be *primordial Being,* the source of all that is and all that has the potential to be. The Son is *expressive Being,* the Word spoken out into the world. The primordial Being pours itself out, sounds through, expressive Being, in the same way that words are an expression of the thoughts in our minds. The Son as expressive Being is the thoughts of God spoken out, even in a human being. The Holy Spirit is *the creative energy of*

Being, the holy breath that forms the words, the builder of form.

We struggle greatly with words and language to describe the Divine and no words can really do justice to the Source of all.

A more down-to-earth and helpful analogy is water. Water is one substance, H_2O – each molecule made of two atoms of hydrogen and one of oxygen. That's what defines what water is. Nothing else is like it. But water can exist in three states – when it's really cold it is a hard solid: ice. Warm it up a bit to get liquid water, or apply more heat to turn it into a gas: water vapour. Now ice is nothing like liquid water – it's hard, it's strong, it floats. But it's still made of the same chemicals, two atoms of hydrogen and one of oxygen. It's still the same stuff. When it's really hot, water turns to vapour – and that you can't even see. There's water vapour in the air all around us. Every time you breathe out, you're breathing out water vapour. It's still H_2O in each case, the same substance, but has very different appearance and properties, depending on which state it is in gas, liquid or solid – but it is still one substance. Likewise, God exists as Father, Son and Holy Spirit – but all are still the One God, still the same substance or essence. So it is with the three faces, or masks, or persons of God. One God, expressed in three ways. God is one essence, One Being, but appears to us in different forms, as does water. Father, Son and Holy Spirit can be a helpful analogy for some, but like any analogy, it is limited.

Deeper Expressions

To take this to a deeper level, there are other, more 'inner' ways of expressing this One in Three, stemming from the Wisdom teachings. God the Father we could see as the masculine aspect, the Will of Being, the driving Power of the Divine that holds the potential for everything to Be. God the Holy Spirit we could see as the feminine aspect, the Creative Being, the Maker of form, the Creator of matter – the Mother aspect of the Divine, a concept which has sadly been lost from Christian tradition. God the Son is then the result of the interaction of the Father and Mother aspects, giving birth to the Love-Wisdom Consciousness, the Christ, the only-begotten Offspring. In human form, the man Jesus of Nazareth had such a level of evolved consciousness that he embodied the Christ consciousness, as much as that is possible for any human being, and became known as Jesus Christ (which should really be expressed as Jesus *the* Christ). But when referring to the only-begotten Son, as in the Nicene Creed, it is the Universal Christ aspect of the Godhead that is being spoken of, not the flesh and blood of Jesus of Nazareth, but the Christ-consciousness that was in him and was him. The American Franciscan Fr Richard Rohr expresses it succinctly in his book *The Universal Christ*:

> Jesus is the union of human and divine in space and time, and the Christ is the eternal union of matter and Spirit from the beginning of time.

This universalisation of the Christ indicates that all matter is anointed in an eternal union. All matter is sustained by the Christ, which could also be identified as the female 'Wisdom' in Proverbs Chapter 8.

> The LORD brought me forth as the first of his works, before his deeds of old; I was formed long ages ago, at the very beginning, when the world came to be. When there were no watery depths, I was given birth, when there were no springs overflowing with water; before the mountains were settled in place, before the hills, I was given birth, before he made the world or its fields or any of the dust of the earth. (Proverbs 8:22–26)

IN the deeper teachings of the Perennial Wisdom, the Universal Christ, the aspect of Love-Wisdom, is the offspring of the Father

Aspect and the Mother Aspect of the Divine. These more inner meanings for the Trinity can be summarised thus:

Father Aspect	Son Aspect Christ	Mother Aspect
Divine Will	Divine Love	Divine Creative Intelligence
Light	Love-Wisdom	Life
Spirit	Consciousness	Matter
Purpose	Evolution	Activity
Cause	Meaning	Effect
I Will to Be	I Am	I Create

So we begin to see other levels of meaning for God that are about the One Life that permeates and holds all in existence, working through created form, energising and inspiring that form in myriads of different ways and paths. These ideas are expanded in the teachings of the Perennial Wisdom, particularly in the more esoteric writings of Alice Bailey and Lucille Cedercrans. This is the Bigger Picture of the Divine Matrix of Being that is large enough to hold the whole universe in existence, with all the billions of stars in each galaxy and the billions of galaxies of unimaginable size to our small human brains. And yet, we are still one with this Divine Being, the One Life which sustains us, that we call God. This is sometimes expressed as *panentheism*, which moves away from the idea that God is 'up there' and we are 'down here'. God is both immanent and transcendent: God is *immanent*, within all of creation, but also *transcendent*, which does not mean 'up there'! It means 'other', lying beyond the ordinary range of human perception. God is within all, holding it all in existence, yet God is still other than material creation. The 'other' is beyond our comprehension, beyond the limits of our most evolved consciousness.

Science speaks of everything in terms of energy. We could also express God in terms of energy. The Deity is essential Life, the sum total of all energies: the energy of Life itself, the energy of Love, the energy of Intelligence, of active experience and that energy which produces the interplay between the seen and the unseen. This is a God transcendent, a God of the immense proportions that the Universe proclaims, and yet still a God immanent, so intimate that we can know the Divine Presence within each one of us.

In answer to the question, 'Who or What is God?' ultimately all we can say is God is Being, God is All, God is the One Life – and that the human race is evolving into deeper levels of consciousness within that One Life.

God is not a being, God is BEING.
God is not a truth, God is TRUTH.
God is not my form, God is FORM.
God is not my feelings, God is LOVE.
God is not my mind, God is MIND.
God is not my life, God is LIFE.
God is not me, God is ALL.
Hence I AM within GOD.

Questions for Discussion

1. Has your understanding of God evolved over time? In what way?
2. How does this view of God sit with your own views?
3. How does this affect your relationship with Jesus the Christ?

Signposts for Further Study
Books

Armstrong, Karen, 1993. *A History of God.* London: Vintage

Barnhart, Bruno, 1999. *Second Simplicity: The Inner Shape of Christianity.* New York: Paulist Press

Bourgeault, Cynthia, 2003. *The Wisdom Way of Knowing.* San Francisco CA: Jossey-Bass

Crawford, Ina, 1990. *A Guide to the Mysteries.* London: The Lucis Press

Nataraja, Kim (ed.), 2011. *Journey to the Heart: Christian Contemplation Through the Centuries.* London: Canterbury Press

Smoley, Richard, 2002. *Inner Christianity: A Guide to the Esoteric Tradition.* Boston MA: Shambhala

Epilogue

'Christianity Expanding' is not an end in itself; it is just a beginning, only dipping a toe in the water! The theology we have inherited has held the shape and form of Christianity faithfully through the ages, but I am suggesting it needs a thorough revision and rethink in the light of modern understandings, and to find a bigger cosmological framework to hold it. The liturgy, hymnody and theology of the Church suffers from exclusivism and archaic views of the nature of divinity, and both of these need to be transcended by concepts more appropriate for today's world. These concepts have to be drawn from the compassionate wisdom of soul level, not from our partial, dualistic, divisive personality level of thinking. Much as St Paul was trying to do in his time and context, we have to put an end to childish ways.

When I was a child, I spoke like a child, I thought like a child, I reasoned like a child; when I became an adult, I put an end to childish ways. For now we see in a mirror, dimly, but then we will see face to face. Now I know only in part; then I will know fully, even as I have been fully known. And now faith, hope, and love abide, these three; and the greatest of these is love. (1Corinthians 13:11–13)

Love is what will abide. Love is the uniting force, the healing energy, that which brings harmony and peace to relationships. It is so much more than a sentimental feeling. It is a force of attraction, bringing everything into ever deeper relationship. It is one of the seven great divine emanations, the Seven Rays known in the Perennial Wisdom teachings, the seven spirits before the throne mentioned in the Bible (Revelation 1:4; 3:1; 4:5; 5:6). Its other aspect is Wisdom, or loving-understanding. The influence of the Ray of Love-Wisdom is growing in our culture today. It is bringing in a new and vital energy that will develop human consciousness and the potential for the human race to live harmoniously with each other and all other life. It is the way forward into the kingdom of God. I believe Christianity has a job of catching-up to do. As a mainstream religion, it has much to offer in terms of providing a path, a way to walk and develop, but it is hampered by its outdated theology and is due for a metamorphic change. If it can expand into the larger cosmic picture presented by both the Wisdom teaching and by science, it can become the Universal Path that I believe Jesus intended it to be. Coming back to the caterpillar analogy of Chapter One, it is time for the chrysalis to break open and the butterfly to emerge and fly into a new dimension.

What Next?

The Wisdom Series of books will gradually introduce the bigger cosmological context which I believe can enhance and support Christianity in the twenty-first century. It will interweave this with new scientific understandings which support this cosmological framework of Perennial Philosophy – the Ageless Wisdom discerned by humanity over aeons. The next book in the series will be about how we use the scriptures, what else should be included, how to understand them and how they can become inspirational without being exclusive. In it, I hope to look afresh at many passages and reinterpret them for today. Following that, we shall look again at the whole Jesus story, and then look at how science and spirituality are on a converging course. I look forward to it!

The Wisdom Series

This book is the first in a series by Revd Don MacGregor, seeking to find new ways of expressing the Christian faith and introduce a new cosmology into which Christianity can expand. The provisional list of other titles to be written is:

Book 2 *Expanding the Scriptures*

How do we understand scripture in this day and age? What about the new texts that have been discovered? How can we reinterpret some old favourite passages?

Book 3 *The Jesus Story*

Jesus and the Christ, the same but different?
The essential message of Jesus.
Jesus was modelling a path of transformation, as Wisdom teacher and trail-blazer.
The wisdom path of initiation modelled by his life story, from Bethlehem to Calvary.

Book 4 *The Science of God: Consciousness*

Quantum physics, Consciousness, Mind before Matter and the holographic nature of the universe held in a Divine Matrix.
Informational domains, morphic fields and collective consciousness.
The power of our minds

Book 5 *The Wisdom Tradition: Awakening*

What is the Wisdom tradition?
Tracing the stream of Wisdom through time.

Book 7 *The Bigger Framework – Perennial Wisdom*

The One Life, Hylozoism, Soul and Personality.
Karma and Reincarnation, Highly Evolved Beings.
The Seven Rays and the planes of existence.

CHRISTIAN ALTERNATIVE
BOOKS

THE NEW OPEN SPACES

Throughout the two thousand years of Christian tradition there
have been, and still are, groups and individuals that exist in
the margins and upon the edge of faith. But in Christianity's
contrapuntal history it has often been these outcasts and
pioneers that have forged contemporary orthodoxy out
of former radicalism as belief evolves to engage with and
encompass the ever-changing social and scientific realities. Real
faith lies not in the comfortable certainties of the Orthodox,
but somewhere in a half-glimpsed hinterland on the dirt track
to Emmaus, where the Death of God meets the Resurrection,
where the supernatural Christ meets the historical Jesus,
and where the revolution liberates both the oppressed and
the oppressors.

Welcome to Christian Alternative... a space at the edge where
the light shines through.
If you have enjoyed this book, why not tell other readers by
posting a review on your preferred book site.
Recent bestsellers from Christian Alternative are:

Bread Not Stones

The Autobiography of An Eventful Life

Una Kroll

The spiritual autobiography of a truly remarkable woman and a history of the struggle for ordination in the Church of England.

Paperback: 978-1-78279-804-0 ebook: 978-1-78279-805-7

The Quaker Way

A Rediscovery

Rex Ambler

Although fairly well known, Quakerism is not well understood. The purpose of this book is to explain how Quakerism works as a spiritual practice.

Paperback: 978-1-78099-657-8 ebook: 978-1-78099-658-5

Blue Sky God

The Evolution of Science and Christianity

Don MacGregor

Quantum consciousness, morphic fields and blue-sky thinking about God and Jesus the Christ.

Paperback: 978-1-84694-937-1 ebook: 978-1-84694-938-8

Celtic Wheel of the Year

Tess Ward

An original and inspiring selection of prayers combining Christian and Celtic Pagan traditions, and interweaving their calendars into a single pattern of prayer for every morning and night of the year.

Paperback: 978-1-90504-795-6

Readers of ebooks can buy or view any of these bestsellers by clicking on the live link in the title. Most titles are published in paperback and as an ebook. Paperbacks are available in traditional bookshops. Both print and ebook formats are available online.

Find more titles and sign up to our readers' newsletter at
http://www.johnhuntpublishing.com/christianity
Follow us on Facebook at
https://www.facebook.com/ChristianAlternative